PETER HURKOS: *I Have Many Lives*

PETER HURKOS:

by NORMA LEE BROWNING

Peter Hurkos: I Have Many Lives
Miller's High Life (with ANN MILLER)
The Honorable Mr. Marigold (with LOUELLA DIRKSEN)
The Psychic World of Peter Hurkos
The Other Side of the Mind (with W. CLEMENT STONE)
Joe Maddy of Interlochen
City Girl in the Country

I Have Many Lives

NORMA LEE BROWNING

DOUBLEDAY & COMPANY, INC.
GARDEN CITY, NEW YORK, 1976

ACKNOWLEDGMENTS

The Columbia Encyclopedia, Second Edition, New York: Columbia University Press, 1950, by permission of the publisher.

"A Bliss Before Dying" by Dr. Russell Noyes, *Newsweek*, May 6, 1974. Copyright 1974 by Newsweek, Inc. All rights reserved. Reprinted by permission.

The Complete Prophecies of Nostradamus, translated, edited, and interpreted by Henry C. Roberts. Copyright 1949 by Henry C. Roberts. Used by permission of Crown Publishers, Inc.

New International Illustrated Encyclopedia of Art. Used by permission of Greystone Press.

"The Mysterious Pyramids" by Max Toth, *Beyond Reality* magazine, December 1972. Reprinted by permission.

Special thanks to my assistants, Vera Servi
and Pam Gallagher, who kept their cool on this psychic
sojourn—and remained as mystified as I am.
And to Tess Damiano for sharing her experiences,
and her tape recorder.

N.L.B.

Library of Congress Cataloging in Publication Data

Browning, Norma Lee.
    Peter Hurkos: I have many lives.

    1. Van der Hurk, Pieter, 1911–   I. Title.
BF1027.V3B69   133.9'3'0924
ISBN: 0-385-01508-9
Library of Congress Catalog Card Number 75–21213

Designed by LAURENCE ALEXANDER

Dedicated to
GLORIA ANN

CONTENTS

When I edited *The Psychic World of Peter Hurkos* (Doubleday, 1970) I wondered what really happened to Peter Hurkos during those four days he lay unconscious in the hospital. Having some knowledge of psychic phenomena, I asked Peter if he had undergone an out-of-body experience; he evaded the question. When the manuscript of this book was delivered to me I discovered that most of it was about those four days and the truly remarkable experience Peter underwent. Now I know there will be some readers who will think this is fiction, that it couldn't possibly have happened, and so be it. As Norma Lee Browning says at one point in the book, "Where did all his visionary experiences come from? The colors, the music, the bearded guides and their gifts? Did they come from other worlds? From previous lives? Of whom? And how? They came from somewhere, and one thing seems fairly certain: they did somehow originate within the biological chemistry of his own brain. He did not manufacture them out of his imagination. He is not that imaginative. They had nothing to do with religious, mystical, or supernatural beliefs. At the time he was devoid of such beliefs."

Although I may not accept everything in the book, I have not made substantial editorial changes—nor did I even suggest any. I know Peter Hurkos and I know him well. He is an admirable man; above all he is an honest man. What he is saying in this book is the truth as he sees it and to me that is justification enough for publishing this book.

The word psychic means less than air to most people. All the same, nobody can deny that without the psyche there would be no world at all, and still less, a human world. Virtually everything depends on the human soul and its functions. It should be worthy of all the attention we can give it, especially today, when everyone admits that the weal or woe of the future will be decided neither by the attacks of wild animals nor by natural catastrophes nor by the danger of world-wide epidemics but simply and solely by the psychic changes in man. . . .

CARL JUNG
The Undiscovered Self

He has the Sun in Taurus, not Gemini, but he does have a Gemini ascendant with Pluto, the most occult of the planets, rising. The chart shows great psychic ability. He likes to touch things because his Sun is in the earth sign of Taurus, which has to do with tangible matter.

Peter Hurkos underwent a process of transformation which had been going on for several years before his accident, although apparently he was not aware of that fact.

At the time of the accident his chart was stretched in every way—to add new dimensions, and for accident and shock. At the time of the accident he "died," and his first reaction to that experience was one of sorrow, profound sorrow. . . .

As for the transformation, on whatever level, I like to describe it with Shakespeare's words:

> Full fathom five thy father lies;
> Of his bones are coral made;
> Those are pearls which were his eyes;
> Nothing of him that doth fade
> But doth suffer a sea-change
> Into something rich and strange.

—RUTH HALE OLIVER
(Noted astrologer and chairman of
the American Federation of Astrologers)

PETER HURKOS: *I Have Many Lives*

{1}

A Ghost from the Past

At the moment of plopping it was black. All black. Then the big searing pyramid of light sucked him up into the other world.

Pieter Cornelis van der Hurk, a house painter from Holland, stood alone and trembling before a celestial jury of nine bearded figures, awaiting their verdict.

They wore long flowing white robes of filmy transparency. Their faces were blurred and shadowy. But their eyes pierced him like sharp beams of hot light. When they spoke, he could see no movement of their mouths. There was only one voice that seemed to come from all of them at once, resounding like an echo in the great domed marble hall. It always came from the direction of a marble throne-chair on an elevated platfom above the jury table. The chair was illuminated by an iridescent triangle of floodlight, but there was no one in it.

"Pieter Cornelis van der Hurk!" the voice rang out. "Peter the Fisherman from Dordrecht . . ."

He looked up at them in fear.

"How do you know I was Peter the Fisherman?" he screamed at them. But no words came out of his throat.

"You are here by mistake," the voice intoned. "It is not your time to die yet. You do not belong here. . . . Your time here is up. . . . We must send you back now. . . ."

"Please don't send me back. I want to stay here. Please don't, *don't*." He was still screaming at them but still nothing came out of his throat.

He bowed his head and began weeping.

"You must be strong," the voice said. "Your work is not finished yet in that other life before death. You were sent here by mistake. You have an important job to do when you go back."

"The only job I know is painting houses!" he cried.

"When you go back, you will not be the same Peter the Fisherman and you will not be a house painter. You will have a great gift from the souls you have met here, and you will have a different kind of job with your gift," the voice said.

"I don't want any gift. I'm so frightened to go back. . . . Please let me stay here," he pleaded.

"Come with us now," the voice said. "And don't be afraid. We will guide you. . . ."

The shadowy figures rose from behind the long marble jury table and said, "Come . . ."

He felt a strange force entering his body, taking possession of him. It was almost as though he were two separate entities, a double being. He tried to speak, to cry out to the bearded images that beckoned him, but the words would not come.

Indistinctly they faded in and out as they led him, and he followed them . . . running, stumbling, crying out to them, trying to reach them . . . until they were gone . . . in nine fast shooting streaks of light, like stars falling in the night.

He was alone now, and there before him was the opening in the mountains with the pyramid of light waiting for him.

He heard a voice say, "Good-by, Peter. Don't be afraid."

He walked into the light and then he felt himself falling again . . . falling, falling. His last thought as he left the other world was, Please don't let me go back to the darkness.

When he awakened he could hear people talking but their voices were like echoes from thousands of miles away. He could see images of people moving all around him but they were blurred and distorted. He could feel someone hold his hand, but he could not talk. His head was racked with pain as sharp as the stabs of knives.

Then, finally, he was able to recognize one of the images. It was a nurse in a white uniform standing beside him, straightening his pillow.

His first words were, "Where am I?"

"You are in the Zuidwal Hospital in The Hague," she said. "And I am your nurse, Nurse Zelda. Do you feel better now?"

She smiled and gently pressed the cool palm of her hand against his burning forehead.

He stiffened and a strange look came into his eyes. Suddenly he grasped her wrist, took her hand from his forehead, held it tightly with both of his hands, and cried out, "Oh, my God! No! No! What I see! What I see! Big fire, explosion! Oh, my God! Be careful! I can't help it . . . !" The words rushed out of him in a strange high-pitched voice that didn't belong to the body of the big Dutchman who lay there writhing in pain. Then he lapsed again into a comatose state.

Nurse Zelda had stood listening to his outburst, terrified.

Then she fled from the room.

I had nearly finished my original manuscript for this book on Peter Hurkos, which was to be an account of his four-day, out-of-body experiences in another world, when a chance meeting with a stranger in a beauty shop took it out of my control. It was as though some mysterious force had wrenched the wheel of a ship from its navigator and steered it off course, into another uncharted direction. And this is not the book it started out to be.

I am not a mystic. I don't believe in these things, certainly not so-called automatic writing. But just as a force moves Peter's fingers over a canvas or the keys of a piano, so it is with me now as I try to reconstruct how it happened, and why.

How many billions of minutes are there in thirty-four years? How can fifteen minutes make such a difference?

Yet, fifteen minutes later I would have missed the oriental lady in the beauty salon who was placed there, I am convinced, at that given time for a purpose.

I had arrived at my beauty shop fifteen minutes early for a ten o'clock appointment. My hairdresser, Bob, was busy with another customer. I changed into a smock and settled myself into the chair next to her to wait my turn. We were the only customers in the shop. It was still very early in the morning for Hollywood, where ladies don't start stirring until noon.

I gave only fleeting notice to the woman in the next chair. She was darkly Asian, with mounds of black hair—and a few strands of gray—which Bob was teasing into a chic, molded bouffant. I pulled out a chapter of my Peter Hurkos manuscript from my tote bag to work on while I was waiting.

Bob glanced over at me and asked, "How are you coming with the Peter Hurkos book?"

"Fine. Almost finished," I mumbled, without looking up, unaware that at this moment the enigmatic something we call fate was intervening.

The woman in the next chair turned sharply toward me and asked, rather awed, "Do you know Peter Hurkos?"

"Yes." I merely acknowledged the question. I was preoccupied with my chapter.

A second later she asked, "Can you tell me how I can get in touch with Mr. Hurkos? I would like very much to see him."

Another weirdo with a problem, I thought. Everybody has problems and they all want Peter Hurkos to solve them.

"I am not permitted to give out his number," I said. I was annoyed at the interruptions. I am not one to strike up conversations in beauty parlors.

But she asked again, this time in a tone of urgency, "Do you *really* know Peter Hurkos?"

I pushed my reading glasses down on my nose, looked over at her intently, for the first time, and said, "Yes, I do know Peter Hurkos. Why do you ask?"

"I would appreciate it very much if you could arrange for me to see him. I really must see him," she said.

She spoke perfect English, with only a trace of an accent. There was an air of mystery and sadness about her and a certain aloofness that puzzled me. She did not fit the mold of those effusive females who are forever hounding Peter for a reading. Yet there was no question about her anxiety to meet him.

"Do *you* know Peter Hurkos?" I asked.

"Yes . . . yes, I know him," she said, looking straight ahead into the mirror. "He's a painter."

This brought me up with a start.

"Are we talking about the same man?" I asked. "Peter Hurkos is a psychic."

"Yes. I know. From Dordrecht." She glanced over at me sideways, quickly, as much as to say, You see. I do know.

"Why do you call him a painter?" I asked.

"Because he is a very fine painter. I have one of his paintings."

"So do I." Peter is a talented painter. It is one of the gifts he brought back from the other world. But he is not known professionally as a painter. "Do you know where he learned to paint?" I asked.

She surprised me by saying, "Of course. In that other world."

"You mean when he was four days dead?"

"Yes. But he was reborn, you know." She said it matter-of-factly, as though everyone should know that. Peter had told me that his parents always said he was "reborn" but I had never heard it from anyone else.

Obviously neither had Bob, our hairdresser. He whirled on his heel with his comb in midair and laughed. "Come on now. What do you mean he was dead and reborn?"

"But it is true," said the oriental lady, still looking straight ahead in the mirror.

I was startled. "How do you know this? Where did you know Peter Hurkos?" I asked.

"He was my patient. . . ."

"Pardon me?"

"He was my patient. I was a nurse on his floor. . . ."

"You mean here, in California, when he had his hip surgery?"

"No, not here. He was my patient in Holland. At the Zuidwal Hospital in The Hague. But I'm sure you never heard of it. That was a long time ago," she said quietly.

I thought I had heard her correctly, but I wanted to be sure. "Did I understand you to say the Zuidwal Hospital?"

"Yes." She looked at me in surprise. "You know Zuidwal?"

"I've heard about it from Peter. You were a nurse there?"

"Yes, an assistant head nurse on Peter's floor."

I was getting goose bumps. I was almost afraid to ask the next question. I didn't want to hear the answer. But I had to ask it. "Was this after his fall?"

"Yes, after his fall. He had a brain injury."

"Yes, I know."

It was on July 10, 1941, that Pieter Cornelis van der Hurk, an apprentice house painter, fell from a ladder, suffered a brain injury, and at first it was thought he would not live. The doctors held no hope for him. He lay unconscious for four days in the Zuidwal Hospital, and when he regained consciousness he was both amnesiac and psychic.

With the help of medical doctors here and in Holland we had obtained the official records from the 'S-Gravenhage Zuidwal Hospital in The Hague for my first book with Peter, *The Psychic World of Peter Hurkos*. There was no question about the records. His case was thoroughly documented. But I had never met any of the doctors or nurses who attended Peter. Many were dead or gone from The Hague. The year 1941 was a long time ago.

Why, at this particular moment in time, nearly thirty-four years later, should the unseen hand of destiny deposit a nurse from the

Zuidwal in the chair next to mine in a beauty shop on Sunset Boulevard and cause me to start rewriting my manuscript?

My own nonpsychic instincts told me that this was what was going to happen. I was annoyed and disturbed at the thought of it.

What hidden secrets were locked inside the oriental enigma sitting next to me?

I studied her face in the mirror. She had small, piquant features and large brown eyes brimming with sadness. Even in her rumpled green and white smock she had an aristocratic dignity and gracefulness. I now guessed her to be Indonesian, since she had lived in Holland. She seemed remote and wrapped up in her own thoughts, as though she no longer wished to pursue the conversation.

But I did.

"Did you get to know Peter very well?" I asked.

"Yes. Oh, yes. . . . At first I was afraid to go into his room. I would only stand in the doorway." She paused, then leaned toward me and added in barely a whisper, as though she didn't want the hairdresser to hear, "He frightened me. . . . He told me too many things." Her eyes clouded with fear at the recollection.

"What kind of things did he tell you?"

She shuddered. "He told me that I would never bury my parents, that I would never see them alive again. And it was true. He told me about the two letters I had in my pocket and about the man I was going to marry. . . . He told me—" She stopped abruptly. Then: "He told me that I am going to die in five years. Now you know why I have to see Peter Hurkos. . . ."

Peter Hurkos never tells anyone when they are going to die.

The oriental lady must be hallucinating. Still, she knew the Zuidwal Hospital and she said she had been a nurse there. "If you know Peter Hurkos," she said, "please tell him you met me. Tell him I was the Indonesian assistant head nurse on his floor. I think he will remember. Tell him I would like for him to come to my house. I will cook an Indonesian dinner for him. And you come, too," she added. "Here, I will give you my card." She reached in her purse for a card. "My number is unlisted but I'll write it for you. Please call me."

The name on the card was Ana Kaneel.

"I live not far from here." It was a good address, one of the best.

Bob had finished her comb-out. She went back to the dressing room and changed into a chic blue jean patchwork pants suit, obviously expensive and well tailored. On the way out, she stopped by my chair, grasped my hand, and said softly, "You know I am an oriental psychic. We understand these things perhaps better than you. . . . Our paths will cross again. I'll be expecting your call."

And she was gone.

"Who is that?" I asked Bob. Hairdressers usually know everything about their clients.

He didn't know much about Ana Kaneel, except that she had been a nurse and had married one of her patients. From her lifestyle he assumed that her husband was wealthy. But he had died recently and she had gone back to nursing part time. That's all Bob knew about her.

"But she's a strange one," he added. "She never talks much and has seemed moody recently. She was supposed to have her hair streaked this morning but she changed her mind at the last minute. Otherwise she would have been under the dryer now and you would have missed her."

As soon as I returned to my apartment, I called Peter's wife, Stephany—Peter never talks on the phone—and told her about Ana Kaneel. The name didn't ring a bell but when I mentioned that she was Indonesian and an assistant head nurse on Peter's floor at the Zuidwal Hospital, Stephy gasped, "Oh, no! She must be that Nurse Zelda we were looking for when we were there. Everyone told us that this nurse was the one we should talk to, but no one could tell us where to find her. They didn't know whether she was dead or alive or where she had gone. But they said she knew Peter better than anyone. . . . Wait till I tell Peter this. I'll call you right back. . . ."

She called back.

"Peter doesn't know any Ana Kaneel [but that wouldn't have been her name anyway] and he doesn't remember any Indonesian nurse [but he was amnesiac in many respects] and he thinks she's a hoax."

"Well, I think we should go and see her anyway," I insisted.

She relayed my message to Peter, came back on the phone and said, "He says he'll think about it. But later. He's busy with the Slasher right now." She was referring to the Los Angeles Skid Row Slasher case which he was working on at the time.

I had an uneasy feeling about Ana Kaneel. But I knew that I would have to see her again.

{2}

The Face in the Clouds

THE FOLLOWING EVENING WE WERE ALL GATHERED AROUND THE BIG
table in the den of Peter's Studio City home—Peter and Stephy
and their new baby, Gloria Ann, in her highchair, the nanny, the
houseboy, Peter's longtime devoted assistant, Tess Damiano, with
the tape recorder, two cats, five dogs, and myself.

We were waiting to watch Peter challenge the Skid Row
Slasher on television.

The Slasher had just murdered his seventh victim. No one since
Charles Manson, who masterminded the Sharon Tate murders,
had set the city so much on edge.

Peter had predicted, just as he had in the Tate case, that the
murderer would strike again unless apprehended soon. The
Slasher case may be solved by the time this is in print. The Los
Angeles Police Department had refused Peter's assistance on the

Slasher case, just as they had on the Tate murders, but Peter had been receiving ominous, threatening calls from someone whom he had reason to suspect was the Slasher, and he had agreed to go on television to challenge him.

Meanwhile, Stephy didn't step out of her front door without her loaded .22 revolver. I didn't much like the idea of her toting it along when she drove me home but she assured me it couldn't go off accidentally and she was considerate enough to keep it pointed in the other direction. The revolver reposed conveniently on the counter beside the TV set, within easy reach if it should be needed on short notice.

Tess was saying, "You know I have always felt that Peter is two different people. When he is working with someone, on a case or a consultation, he is an entirely different person from the one who is sitting here and talking to us now."

Peter sat with his back to the waning sunlight. His arms rested on a colorful Persian rug spread over the table, and he nervously flicked his cigar and tapped his big fingertips as he talked. Behind him, through the sliding glass doors and windows, and beyond the swimming pool and guest house, lay the steeply terraced two-acre hillside with the stair-step rows of gardens that Peter had planted. They were his pride and joy. Peter was saying, "You know I talk to my plants every day. I talk to my string beans, they are beautiful. Soon I bring you string beans and tomatoes from my garden. . . . Everything has a soul, you know, plants, vegetables, trees, flowers, everything. You know what I want to do with myself in this life, if I did not have my gift? What I would want is to be in the mountains with nature and flowers, and create paintings and playing music . . . and live all the lives I had before. . . ."

It was like a monologue, almost as though he were talking to himself with no one else present. His deep dark eyes, with a filmy radiance emanating from them, seemed to glaze over and look far past and beyond us, as though seeing something that we could not see. Though he would deny it, they were the eyes of a man in trance as he continued his soliloquy:

"All people have had other lives. . . . I have many lives. . . . I was many different people. . . . I have never studied the piano, the organ, or painting. . . . That was my gift when I fell from the ladder. I never played the organ or painted before, so how could I learn? I must be many different people in other lives. How can I rub my fingers across an envelope like this [he demonstrates] and see what is inside? Because I did it somewhere before, in another life. How do you think I walk out of my body and watch my own operation. The Voice tells me. . . . How do you think I know what to eat and learn to heal myself? The Voice tells me. . . ."

"Where does the Voice come from, Peter?" I asked, knowing what his answer would be.

"From that other world, where I was when I fell from the ladder. That's where I went . . . where I met all the little people and the man with the beard. . . . When I come back even my own mother and father did not recognize me. They say I was reborn. I'm reborn with two minds and the Voice that won't go away. I would be so happy if I could switch it off."

He slammed the palm of his hand on the table and railed at himself, "You know why this happen to me? It's my punishment. YOU DO BAD THINGS AND BAD COMES BACK TO YOU. YOU DO GOOD THINGS AND GOOD COMES TO YOU. I learn that from my fall. That's why they sent me back from the other world, why they would not let me stay. . . . They tell me it's my punishment."

"Who told you that?" I asked.

"The Voice! How many times do I have to tell you this? I always tell you the Voice but nobody believes me. They think I'm mental cuckoo. . . ." He tapped his head with his fingers.

"Do you really believe you were on another planet, or in another world?" I asked.

"Are you kidding? I know I was! I can prove it." He was beginning to get angry.

I tried to calm him. "Peter, have you ever heard of something called out-of-body travel?"

"No. What's that?"

"I think it may be the experience you had, the way you describe it."

"I don't know what you are talking about," he said. "But I know I walked out of my own body and watched my operation. And I left my body when I had my fall and the light sucked me up to that other planet."

The television had been turned down low while we waited for Peter's appearance. I was across the table, facing Peter, with my back to the TV set. Suddenly he halfway stood and lunged over the table, angrily jabbing his finger toward the television.

"There's the person who said my gift was from the devil!" He was livid with rage. "Look at the face, look at the eyes, look at the mouth. A very bad person."

We all looked at the face on the TV screen. It was one of those religious fanatics leading another crusade. Tess turned the TV up, but Peter's voice drowned out the crusader.

"Look at it . . . all that yelling! Fanatical. You call that religion?

"It's all for money. . . . I could be rich too if I wanted to build a church and have a cult and prove my gift. Sure, I could preach my own religion and be very rich. But I would be a hypocrite. . . ."

"Peter, where did you meet that evangelist?" I asked.

"With a friend of mine in 1959. My friend was talking about my gift and that preacher said, 'This gift is from the devil,' and I asked where the preacher got this information. I said, 'I can prove something with my gift, what can you prove?' Anybody can read the Bible, many ways. The Bible was written symbolically not by one person but by many people, by psychic people. . . . You call them prophets. . . ."

There was a swell of religious music in the background as the crusader continued.

"Turn it off!" Peter thundered. Then toward the empty TV screen he grumbled, "I can prove my gift is not from the devil, can you?"

Tess turned the television on again when it was time for the news program with Peter on the Slasher. . . . Then we returned to the subject of his "gift," as he always calls it.

"My gift is not from the devil," he said, still grumbling at the preacher. "It is from the men I saw up there—with the beards. Here, come, I show you a painting and prove it to you where my gift come from."

Two large rooms of Peter's home—the living room and the one he calls his "organ room," dominated by his $10,000 electric organ —are covered from floor to ceiling with his oil paintings, all done with great globs of paint rolled on with his hands and fingers. He never uses a brush. I had seen his paintings many times before but had not paid particular notice to them, except a few that he had painted especially for me.

"When did you first learn to paint?" I asked.

"I told you, I never study, I learn it up there, in that other world. How many times do I have to tell you?"

"But I mean—when did you first start painting down here, in this world? Did you ever do any paintings in Holland, before you came to America?"

"No. Never. Here was first."

·"Then how did the Indonesian lady know you were a painter?"

"What Indonesian lady?"

"The nurse from the Zuidwal, the one we told you about. She wants us to come and see her," I reminded him. "She says she has one of your paintings."

"She must be crazy lady." Then he said:

"I don't know any nurse from the Zuidwal. I never did any paintings in Holland. Never. Only for my sister when I was there three years ago. All the others I do here. Look at them. . . ."

We were in the organ room now. "Come, I will show you a painting that will give you goose pimples. I painted a face that was from one of the men—and he was a child, too."

"What man?"

"Come on, I show you."

He led us into their bedroom and up to a small painting that hung on the north wall. The room, done in deep purple, from carpeting to bedspread and drapes, was Stephy's artistic handiwork, but the painting was unmistakably Peter Hurkos . . . a small, dark, brooding scene of woods and trees and a winding pathway— or was it a stream?—leading upward and into a troubled sky filled with clouds. There was the touch of turbulence that haunts most of Peter's paintings. In the pale lavender glow of light there was a rather ghoulish feeling about it—or was it an aura?—as though it had materialized ethereally from some other world.

I said to myself, You're going cuckoo, too. You've been around Peter Hurkos too long.

To Peter I said, "It's beautiful. It has an other-worldly quality. The clouds are so strange. Why do you always paint clouds like that?"

He did not answer. Instead, he took a few steps over to his left and said, "Now come and stand by me, and look at it from here. What do you see?"

I had been standing close-up with my nose on the painting, studying it. The title on the small plaque was "Mur Woods." I took a long last look at it, making a mental note of everything . . . the shape of the trees, the white-ribboned pathway through the woods, the clouds. . . . Then I went over and stood beside Peter and I saw it—a little boy's face in the clouds. He had black curly hair and a white floating scarf of clouds around his neck. His head was tilted slightly, and there was a faint, peaceful smile on his face. . . . He seemed to be looking right at us, or through us. . . .

"I don't believe it," I said. I stepped over to another position and the little boy was gone. But when I came back to Peter's side, he was there.

It was the same with Tess. She saw it as clearly as I did. "In all the years I have worked with Peter," she said, "he has never shown me this painting. I have seen it before, but I always thought of it as just 'Mur Woods'—the trees and the clouds."

"Now, I want to show you something else," Peter said. "Come over here. What do you see now?"

Above the little boy's head we saw the shadowy but distinct form of another face. For a second there was dead silence. Tess and I at the same time recognized the face that Peter had told us about.

"That's the man with the *beard!*" we both said at once.

"Right," said Peter. "The man with the beard. When he was young and when he was old."

Hmmm. I squinted, stepped this way and that, looked at it again and again, then said skeptically, "Ver-rr-y clever! How did you manage to do that, Peter?"

"Are you kidding! Ask Stephy! I didn't see it till three weeks after I finished. It was hanging there and one night I was here in the bed and I woke up and I put on the light, and I saw him there. I woke up Stephy and I said, 'My God, that's him, the man I saw from that other world. Same face, same beard. . . .'

"Ask anybody! Other people saw it. I didn't see it alone. I showed it to many people and they all saw it, same as you. Some people offer me a lot of money for it, and I wouldn't sell it. . . . This is my proof, where my gift comes from. . . . The man with the beard, and when he was a boy. . . ."

"Could we take it down, move it into another light?" I suggested.

"Sure. I show you." He carefully lifted the painting from its hook on the wall, carried it into the den, and placed it in first one spot, then another. At some angles we could see only the woods, the winding pathway, the turbulent clouds. But at other angles, when the light was right, we could all see clearly, distinctly, unmistakably, the little boy's face in the clouds—and the shadowy face with the beard just above him.

The man's face looked distorted, anguished. His mouth was upturned and open, as though crying out for something, or in pain. One arm, formed of clouds, was around the boy.

Even the nanny could see it. She cried, "*Mi Dios,*" then lifted baby Gloria Ann from her highchair and quickly left the room.

Everyone has seen, from an airplane or from down here, on earth, "pictures" of people, animals, and imaginary scenes in formations of clouds. They linger for a while, then they move and are gone.

But Peter's painting of "Mur Woods" remained the same. The face in the clouds would not go away.

"When did you paint it?" I asked.

"About three years ago . . ."

"Did you know what you were doing when you painted it?"

"No. I did it all with my fingers. Look, you can see my fingers on top of the clouds."

"What did you start out to paint—a picture of the woods?"

"No, the clouds. I always start with the clouds." There was deep sadness in his voice.

"You were not thinking of painting a boy—or a man with a beard?"

"NO! I tell you NO! I only saw that later, when I was finished. My hands only go where the force tells me to go. The force wants me to do it. . . . My hands have to do it. . . .

"And I am not a painter, I am not an artist. . . . I was only a house painter. . . ."

"When you say force, Peter, do you mean the Voice?"

"No, no, no. The Voice I hear only when I work on cases, and talk to my plants, and walk out of my body. But the Voice doesn't come when I paint, only the pictures. And then the force that makes my hands move, like when I play the organ. It is all in my mind first, from up there, that other world. . . . Come here. Look!"

He led us back into the organ room with all his paintings. "You see all those clouds? But you don't see faces in the clouds. All the hundreds of paintings I've done, they never come out like this one. . . . I was painting double . . . and I didn't know it. . . . and then I see something else in it that I didn't want. . . . I looked at it and I said, 'Oh, my God, that's the person I saw up there on trial . . . when I was on trial. . . .' "

"You said there were nine men on the jury?"

"Yes, nine. But all look the same. Same beard, same voice. Down here I see only one, hear only one, but it's from all of them."

Peter studied his "Mur Woods" painting again, and said to himself, "My God, what a beautiful face, the little boy. Half dark, half light . . . but it comes out so clear. . . .

"I'm tired now. I need rest."

He abruptly excused himself, leaving us mystified by "Mur

Woods." Its title, Tess suggested, should be changed to "The Face in the Clouds."

Stephy objected. "It's my picture and my title," she said. "Peter painted it especially for me because it's a real place where we were once, a redwood forest, and it was so beautiful I think the title should be the same as the name of the place, 'Mur Woods.'"

Stephy had misspelled the name. Actually, it is Muir Woods, a beautiful state forest of redwoods not far from San Francisco. But the name on the little plaque she had made for it was "Mur Woods" and that's how it will be known here.

Anyone can find hidden images in many paintings, if we squint hard and long enough, this way or that, in a certain light. But in "Mur Woods" why couldn't we have found a flying horse or an elephant? Why did it have to be a boy's face in the clouds and Peter's "man with the beard" from the other world?"

{3}

Leaving My Body

THE LITTLE BOY'S FACE IN THE CLOUDS HAUNTED ME. NOT SO MUCH the other face with the beard, but the boy's face. He looked vaguely familiar. Somewhere I had seen that face before, and I had a strange feeling that I would see it again.

The more I thought about it, the more certain I was that it was the face of a boy genius we all know, or more probably the face of a famous person as a child—from the long-ago past.

I recruited a crew of helpers to start tracking down childhood pictures of great men of the past in their own or public libraries. I asked them to start with composers and painters.

I did not tell Peter or Stephy about this project. They were much more concerned with the other face, the one Peter always refers to as the man with the beard, or sometimes the Voice with the beard.

More often he speaks only of the Voice, a voice that is very real to him and which apparently has dominated his life ever since his return from that out-of-body trip to another world. It is this Voice that guides him when he plants his gardens. . . . It is the Voice he hears when he is working as a psychic detective on missing persons or murder cases.

And the same Voice was with him when he sat up in his hospital bed and said to Stephy, "I am going to live," then proceeded to leave his body and watch his hip operation.

Again, as with the strange and sudden appearance of a nurse from the Zuidwal, there was a curious juxtaposition of time that puzzled me. Peter entered the Marina Mercy Hospital at Marina Del Rey, California, on September 5, 1973.

As I wrote that date a memory switch clicked to another, August 5, 1941, the date Peter was released from the Zuidwal.

Turn the clock back to that sunny afternoon in The Hague, Holland, when a handsome young house painter with black curly hair and flashing dark eyes lost his footing and plunged from the top of a four-story building to the concrete pavement below.

It was approximately five o'clock in the afternoon when Peter Hurkos left his body to begin his journey into the unknown, that nebulous nether world between life and death. When he returned, he was no longer the happy man of the flashing dark eyes but a total stranger to himself and everyone else, a man tortured with two minds inhabiting the same body.

He was "sentenced" to this earthly "jail," as he calls it, on the date of his discharge from the Zuidwal, August 5, 1941.

Exactly thirty-two years and one month later, to the very day, and four thousand miles across the sea, he was admitted to the Marina hospital where he would soon be released from his earthly "jail" and leave his body again for a brief visit to that other world where he was after his fall.

It is even possible that his psychic entities met each other coming and going between worlds, for philosophers tell us that in the abstract universe there is no time as we know it.

Was it sheer coincidence that brought the Indonesian nurse, Ana Kaneel, into our lives by a hair's-breadth of fifteen minutes in thirty-four years? Was it sheer coincidence that timed Peter's second out-of-body experience so close to his first? Or did his man with the beard plan it that way? These are questions for the philosophers who deal in the abstract universe. I am no philosopher. I am merely a chronicler of the strange events and circumstances that seem always to surround Peter.

It was six o'clock in the morning when Peter bolted upright in his hospital bed and tapped Stephany, who was dozing in a chair at his bedside.

"Wake up, Stephy, wake up! I want you to go order flowers—two dozen red roses. Quick! I need them. Now!"

Stephy yawned, sleepily, then roused herself enough to be concerned. This was the day of his operation. They had spent two restless, sleepless nights worrying about it. Peter had been unusually depressed. He had even hinted to Stephy that he might not pull through, and for the past several days his psychic gift seemed to have deserted him.

"Why do you want flowers now, Peter? You're not going to die, you're going to be all right," Stephy said, trying to comfort him.

As it happened, Peter didn't need comfort. He had just had a good session with the Voice.

"I am not going to *die*, I am going to *live*," Peter said. "And I am going to walk again in fourteen days. The Voice told me. It's the truth, he told me I am going to heal myself." Peter almost shouted in excitement.

"When did the Voice tell you that?" Stephy asked.

"Just now. A while ago. I tried to sleep but I could not. Then the Voice comes, clear as anything. He tells me I'm not going to die!"

"Then why do you need all these flowers, now, dear?" Stephy asked.

"Because I'm going to need them for smell, for oxygen. They help me heal faster. I want you to go and order two dozen red roses to be sent to this hospital room every day I am here. Standing order, you hear?" It was a command.

"But, Peter, the shops aren't even open yet. Do you know what time it is?" she reminded him.

"Okay. But go as soon as they open, and remember, standing order every day," Peter instructed. "The doctors, too," he added. "Send them the best, most expensive flowers you can find to thank them, because I'm going to come out of it all right. But for me—two dozen red roses every day. . . ."

"You'll be getting tons of flowers from friends. You won't have room for all of them. Why order them for yourself?" Stephy asked, always the practical one.

"Never mind, never mind. Just do what I say. I need the red roses for smell, for breathing, for energy," Peter explained impatiently. Stephy promised she would go for the flowers as soon as the shops opened. . . .

At nine o'clock Peter was wheeled into the operating room for major hip surgery. (His hip had been injured in a climbing accident while working on a case.)

He does not know the exact time when he left his body but he distinctly remembers that he stood in the doorway, white-gowned and smiling, as he watched a team of surgeons sawing into his hip bone.

"I know I was out [under anesthesia], but I saw my own body lying there on the table. I watched the whole operation. At first I was afraid. I thought they were sawing off my leg. I said, I want my leg, and I want my hip, don't take my leg off.

"But then I was not afraid any more because the Voice was there. . . . He was telling me that everything was going to be all right, and it was. I healed myself. I walked in fourteen days. I told the doctors when I came out from the operation that I was going to walk in fourteen days. They said it was impossible. . . . But I did. Ask the doctors. . . ."

The doctors and nurses did indeed confirm not only Peter's speedy recovery for an operation of this type* but also his rather peculiar behavior at times. Most medical people are reluctant to use the word "psychic" but they were amazed (and probably amused) at some of Peter's seemingly unexplainable "aberrations" —such as his insistence on being taken straight from the operating room to his own room rather than a recovery room (normal operating procedure); his refusal to permit any of the bowers of flowers to be removed from his room ("I am breathing my life from them," he insisted); and his predilection for telling others what was happening to patients in the rooms next to and across the hall from his, not to mention his psychic readings of some of the doctors and nurses themselves.

Peter, of course, did not tell them about hearing the Voice.

"If they think I hear voices, they would lock me up as a mental case, cuckoo." He always says this tapping his forefinger on his forehead.

In our earlier sessions, Peter had been reluctant to talk even to me about the Voice. It was not until much later, and after years of constant questioning—which he at times resented—that I was able to extract from him anything more than mere moody mumblings about the "voice," which we eventually came to speak of freely with at least an anonymous identity as the Voice. And it wasn't until much later, after considerable prodding, that he identified the Voice as belonging to that "man with the beard." In fact, it was during one of our early sessions on his out-of-body experience at the Marina Del Rey hospital that he first mentioned the man with the beard. I had been interrogating him about the voice.

"You said the Voice was there with you when you watched your operation. Was it just a voice that you heard in your ears or your head, Peter, or was it the voice of someone you knew, or a person you could see?"

* Dr. Marshall R. Urist, specialist in orthopedic surgery, has used Peter in his lectures as an example of how mind power can aid in speedy recovery.

"Just the Voice," he said, and his own voice at the time was one that came from the depths of a man in anguish. He did not look at me. His head was bent slightly downward as he flicked an ash from his cigar into an ashtray, and his eyes, vacant and staring, seemed to be fixed on some mesmerizing spot in the Persian rug on the table. He stared at it a long time, and none of us disturbed him.

Finally he raised his head and with a heavy sigh he blurted out, "I have to tell you what I saw. It was that man from the other world, the man with the beard. He was with me when I saw my operation. He was standing there with me all the time. Then he said, 'Now you don't need me any more, you are going to heal yourself.' And he went away. It was the same man, same voice, same beard. . . . But it is the Voice that I hear all the time from when I fall off the ladder. If I could switch it off, I would be the most happy man in the world. But it is always there. . . ."

This was my first real introduction to the man with the beard. Peter had told us about watching his operation long before he showed us the "Mur Woods" painting.

At first, I had thought Peter was either hallucinating, fabricating, or capitalizing on some popular pseudo-religious concepts.

Anybody could guess who his man with the beard was.

"God or Jesus or somebody like that?"

"NO! NO! NO!" he roared, pounding both fists on the table. "Don't you understand, it is NOT religious! My gift is not from God or the devil, it is from those men up there on the jury who gave me the Voice. . . ."

"What did this man with the beard look like?" I asked.

"I don't know. I never saw his face. He was like a shadow, and transparent, too, like all the others up there. . . ."

"You mentioned a jury—up there. Nine men?"

"Nine. Only nine." He was quite definite about it. "All with beards, very intellectual, all the same voice. . . ."

"And it is the same voice you hear down here when you're doing murder cases? You are positive?"

"Always the same."

"Have you ever had any other out-of-body experiences?" I asked.

"What do you mean, out-of-body?" He still didn't comprehend. "No, I only leave my body twice, once when I fell and here, with the operation. That's all. No more. . . . But I saw my mother when she came to me out of her body, also twice, two times I saw her. . . ."

Peter told us about it.

He was doing a demonstration for a college audience in Tampa, Florida, one night when he suddenly broke out in a cold sweat and cried, "Stop! I have to stop. I see my mother in a casket with yellow flowers." He composed himself, then continued his show, but as soon as it was finished, about 11 P.M., he called his wife in Miami and asked, "Have you heard anything from my mother? Is something wrong?" His wife said no. But by the time he arrived home the next day, the cablegram from Amsterdam had arrived. His mother had died—and at approximately the same moment he saw her in his stage demonstration. He called his sister in Amsterdam and asked, "Did mother have yellow flowers in her hands?" His sister said yes. She also confirmed other details that Peter knew despite the seven thousand-mile distance and nine-hour time difference.

"How do you explain that?" he asked. It is a question many before have asked.

The other time when he saw his mother was during a screening of the film *The Great Caruso* at his home in Studio City.

"My mother loved that picture," he recalled. "I went with her to see it three times in The Hague. So, many years later I rented the film just to see it again because my mother loved it so much.

"I was sitting in the big chair [in the living room] watching it, and then I saw a flash, like a light from a car through the window. Then I see my mother, and she looked at me and smiled. I thought, There must be something wrong. So I stood up and I went over there, to the other side of the room, and I didn't see anybody, *Nobody!* But I sat down again and I saw my mother again. Then I went out for Stephy. I told her, 'I just saw my mother, she was sitting on the couch, I saw her black curly hair and she smiled at me.' . . . Stephy didn't believe me. . . ."

I wasn't sure I believed him, either.

"Are you sure it was your mother, Peter?"

"What the hell! Don't you think I know my own mother? But I saw it all in a flash. I saw her, I know I saw her, and then when I stood up and left and then came back to the chair where she was, nothing was there. . . . I saw *The Great Caruso* three times with my mother. . . . I got sick and tired of it . . . but that's when I saw my mother again, in my own living room, sitting on the couch, when I was showing *The Great Caruso* that she loved. . . ."

The time had come when I had to take Peter back to the beginning. There were too many questions left unanswered, doors unopened.

Time and again, quizzing Peter about that crucial moment in his life when he fell to what should have been an early death, I had run up against a stone wall.

What did he remember from those four days of unconsciousness? Nothing. Where had the gift come from? A shrug. Or "up there." Why did his mother say, "This is not our Pieter who comes back to us—it is someone else?"

Peter's inability to explain these circumstances had left him at least as frustrated as I was in trying to get at the truth of them.

I finally said to Peter, "Let's go back to the beginning. You remember your fall, right?"

"Are you kidding? It is just like it happened today. I'll never forget it."

"Would you be willing to relive it—under hypnosis?"

"No! No! Never! Nobody else touch my brain now. I got the voices, the pictures. . . . I have enough with my brain already! I don't need nobody else messing with it! I don't want any hypnosis."

For some reason Peter had acquired a deep-seated fear of anything associated with witchcraft or the occult. For him hypnosis fell in this category, and he could not tolerate the word "trance." He will go into a rage when this is read to him—he reads only in his native Dutch, so Stephy and I must read his book to him, chapter by chapter—but it is nevertheless true, whether he realizes it or not, that Peter's gift works best when he is in a state of semihypnotic trance, or sometimes, perhaps, total self-hypnosis.

He doesn't believe this at all, and I have long since given up arguing with him about it.

If he wouldn't do it under hypnosis, I asked, could he possibly remember, recapture, and relive it all just for the tape recorder? "Maybe," he said. "I try."

{4}

The Fall

IN ALL THE YEARS I HAD KNOWN PETER, AND IN ALL THE TIME WE
had worked together on his first book, there remained with me
the gnawing frustration that I really didn't know him at all.

He could be pressed only so far and then the veil fell, an inscrutable veil that was impossible to penetrate.

Who was this man who said he had come back from another
world with a "gift"—a gift which in Holland was to become
known as "*het derde oog,*" "the third eye," and, in America, as a
"sixth sense"? A gift accompanied by voices and visions that
somehow endowed him with psychic powers. . . . A gift of
rebirth into a man with a "double mind" and three amazing
talents—painting, music, and clairvoyance. . . . A third eye
which could "see" things that his own two eyes have never seen
and his conscious mind knows nothing about. . . .

He had once tried to describe to me his feelings and what he saw when he was falling from the ladder, but the memory of it was too painful. He had described that "other world" of his unconsciousness only as being very beautiful, filled with music and color. He had spoken reluctantly of the voices—or voice—and the pictures that came to him out of nowhere. . . . But I always sensed that there was something he was holding back.

I felt certain that if only he would consent to hypnosis, it would unlock some of these mysteries and tell us much more about Peter Hurkos. But he remained adamantly resistant to this, in the morbid fear of anyone "messing" with his mind.

Now, finally, he had agreed to let me try to take him back to the beginning, from the moment he fell. He would try to relive those four days during which he had left his body after the fall.

There were many times during the weeks that followed when he faltered and broke off emotionally, saying he couldn't go on. There were times when he became irritable and agitated at our questions; for Stephany and Tess, taking turns at the tape recorder, were as baffled as I was at some of his strange outpourings. It became obvious that Stephy, despite the special bond of closeness between them, was hearing much of her husband's story for the first time.

It is important for readers to know at the outset that Peter's understanding of the English language is limited; he still speaks with a heavy Dutch accent, broken grammar, mixed tenses, and a child's grasp of the literal meaning of many words and phrases that are familiar to most of us. As much as possible, I have tried to capture the flavor and nature of Peter's mental processes—important for serious students of pyschic phenomena—by using material taken verbatim from the transcripts of our tape-recording sessions, with only minor changes of grammatical construction, not of content, to make it easier for our readers.

I first explained to Peter what I wanted to do, and I asked him again whether he really wanted to go ahead with it. "Ya, okay," he shrugged. I told him that I would be asking many questions. Only he knew the answers, and some might be painful for him to remember. I especially warned him that I was going to ask him to remember all the details about his fall. Did he feel like talking about it?

He was silent a moment. Then he said, "I try. We see."

I asked him to close his eyes and relax and make his mind blank for a while. He seemed uncomfortable. So I told him that if he didn't feel like doing it now, we would wait until another time. "No," he said, resigned. "We start now."

I knew that something was hurting him deeply, but I also knew that it had to come out of him and we might as well get it over with.

Now, Peter, we are going back to those four days when you were unconscious, out of your body, and in that other world you've talked about—where you said it was so beautiful.

"Yes, so beautiful, I want to go back, I want to stay there," he interrupted, brusquely.

But first we have to find out how you got there. You have to remember every single detail of it, from the time you fell off the ladder. I want you to go back now to that day, July 10, 1941. Do you remember it?

"Do I remember it? How could I forget it? The fall, it is just like it happened today. Yes, I think about it many times. And I see the whole thing clearly. I am up there on the ladder between two windows. My father gave me the upper stories to paint. He was painting down below. I was not so good a painter as my father, but he says, 'Who cares about the roof if it looks nice down below?' So he gave me the high part only.

"I was reaching over for my paint bucket and I slipped. Then I was falling, falling, and I thought I am going to die, and I DON'T WANT TO DIE, I WANT TO LIVE! I am fighting, fighting, from the moment I was falling down from the ladder, because I didn't want to die. Then it was black, for a long time black. I am in darkness. The people who saw me falling told the doctors that I got up and walked eight or ten feet and then collapsed. But the last thing I remember thinking is, Please God, I DON'T WANT TO DIE. Then there was the darkness, and then there was the light that took me up to the other world, like suction. . . ."

Wait a minute, Peter, what else were you thinking or feeling and what did you actually see during that time when you were falling? You had a wife, then, remember? Weren't you thinking about her, or your children, or your mother and father? Try to remember what else you were thinking, and everything you saw when you were falling. You must have thought about your family.

"No, no. Not my mother, not my father . . ." He spoke haltingly. A physical change came over him. He seemed unaware that anyone else was in the room. He did not look up. He sat like a man transfixed in aloneness and pain. None of us spoke, until finally I broke the silence, gently.

I think there was something else you wanted to say, Peter. Don't be afraid. Who were you thinking about, who did you see when you were falling?

"Tommy. Just Tommy, that's all I saw. Not my mother, not my father, not my wife, just Tommy." His voice was choked.

Tommy?

Stephy and Tess and I exchanged silent, puzzled expressions. None of us had ever heard of Tommy.

And from the emotional state Peter was in, I decided it was best for us all to take a coffee break before pursuing the subject of Tommy any further.

Peter was unusually quiet during the interlude, turning now and then to hug one of his dogs. He was especially fond of the big one, Max, who was old and lame now.

"I think Max won't be with us much longer," Stephy said. But they were always taking in strays, the latest a half poodle, half something else, female, with epilepsy and emaciated. Peter and Stephy had nursed her back to health and had her epilepsy well under control.

I finally asked Peter if he felt like talking any more tonight or would he prefer to wait for another time.

"Yes, we finish now," he said abjectly, as though it were a burden to unload, and then forget.

You were talking about Tommy, the only person you saw when you were falling. Was he—someone in your family—or close to you? Who was Tommy?

"Yes, Tommy was very close to me. Closer than any of my family." He faltered again.

"Tommy was my dog. . . . And when I was falling from the ladder, I saw what I did. I killed my dog Tommy. I am falling, falling, and I am fighting, I DON'T WANT TO DIE. . . . But I know this is my punishment, because I killed my dog Tommy. It is bad to hurt someone . . . and Tommy was the only friend I had in this world. . . . I never have told this to anyone else. Never! But Tommy was all I saw when I fell from the ladder. . . . Not my mother, not my father, but my dog Tommy. . . ."

You won't ever have to say it to anyone else, Peter. Why was Tommy so special to you . . . and . . . why . . . how did you kill him?

"I drown him. I threw him over the bridge. And when I was falling, I saw his eyes looking up at me through the foam, and I knew this was my punishment, that I had to die because I have killed my dog Tommy."

How old were you when you killed your dog Tommy?

"About eleven."

And you were thirty when you had your fall?

"Yes. All these years I never forgot. It was my punishment."

How long did you have Tommy? Why did he mean so much to you? Why do you have such strong feelings about him?

This obviously was a very painful subject for Peter. He had kept it bottled up inside of him, and then slowly, reluctantly, for the first time, the deep-throated words tumbled out of him, sometimes with tears brimming in his eyes:

"Tommy was my dog. My dog. But he was more than my dog. He was my friend, my only friend . . . a very close friend. I had him since I was six years old. He was a mixed dog, between a Schnauzer and a poodle. We call it a street dog. . . . And he loved to swim . . . always swimming with me in the river. . . .

"You see, I was a black sheep from the beginning. I was a strange boy. I was born a strange boy. Maybe I had my gift before, but I didn't know. Everybody needs somebody, but nobody wanted me. I had not much schooling, not much mother love or father love. . . . And children didn't want to play with me when I was a kid. So I found my love by nature, by animals, by a dog . . . a dog that I destroyed. . . . Why was it my mother didn't give me love? Why my brother and not me? I always did wrong. . . . Why didn't my father make a living for my mother? Why did I have to steal vegetables from other people? When I disappeared, my mother didn't even report it that I was gone. Why . . . ?

"Why was it that kids wouldn't play with me? What was wrong with me? Why do I have to be alone? So I go with my dog, and we go where nobody is, always alone. In school I was always staring. I could learn very well but my mind was always in another world. Why?"

Peter, why are you questioning yourself with whys?

"Why? I have never understood those whys. There is no answer to any of them. I finally said, forget all those whys.

"Then I lived just with my dog, Tommy. He was my friend, everything I had. I had Tommy for about six years. He was always with me.

"I had a canoe and I was stealing fruit. I went to all the rich houses, and I saw peaches and I saw cauliflower, and we didn't have any money, and my dog Tommy was always with me in the canoe when I was stealing the fruit.

"My father was making three guilders a week as a house painter, and he had four children. Rent was one guilder and fifty cents, and there wasn't much for food. We had to go to the fields and pick the corn that was left, and my mother baked all our bread, but we were poor and we were hungry. I couldn't take it.

"There were so many rich people there in town, and so many beautiful fruits and vegetables, so I bought this canoe for two guilders and I repaired it because it was leaking, and I would take Tommy with me and we went and loaded my canoe right up to the top until it almost sank. Then I sold the fruit for five cents a kilo, and I came home with about two and a half guilders. I was making almost as much as my father. So I gave it to my mother, and my mother thought I was in business. But nobody ever found out.

"I saw all of this during my fall, yes. But mostly what I saw was my dog Tommy. . . . Tommy and I were playing with my sister, Allie, in an open field about a mile away from our house. It was kind of a junkyard where Tommy loved to chase rats. I don't know what happened. I think maybe he went wild. He bit my sister, a whole big chunk out of her leg, and she was bleeding badly. Some people came and helped my sister and drove her in a buggy to the doctor. . . . I was so confused when I saw my sister bleeding that I went screaming for Tommy. . . . And I took a big cloth and put him in it, and I tied a big stone around his neck, and I threw him over the bridge.

"I can still see it . . . the foam coming out of his mouth and his eyes looking up at me . . . and then I tried to jump in after him . . . but it was too late. . . .

"I said to my mother, I punished the dog, I killed him. And my mother wasn't mad about it at all. She said, 'Good.' And my father wasn't mad. Nobody was mad that I killed my dog. Nobody told me it was wrong. But I knew it was wrong, and I was very hurt. I couldn't sleep for three days at home, I was out looking for Tommy. I was seeing his eyes and his legs paddling when I threw him over. . . . And I was deeply hurt. . . . But it was too late.

"Tommy was the only dog I ever had as a child. He was the only animal that I ever killed. I never hurt another animal. I love animals. Why did I do this to Tommy?

"I saw it all clear during my fall. . . . My dog Tommy was sinking, and I was having the same feeling of sinking. . . . When I was falling I couldn't breathe. . . . I was like Tommy, with the rope and the stone around him. . . . And I saw his eyes when I looked over the bridge. . . . No one told me it was wrong. But I knew. I saw it all when I was falling. . . . The only real sin is when you hurt someone. . . . And I knew this was my punishment. . . . Now, I am going to die for what I have done to Tommy. . . ."

Peter, how long do you think it took you to fall?

"I don't know how long it took, maybe fifteen seconds in the falling, about forty-five feet . . . and I was fully conscious when I was falling. . . .

"And I didn't care about my family. . . . All I could think about was Tommy and I DON'T WANT TO DIE. . . . Then everything went black."

Peter's biggest ordeal was over, finished. I would never mention Tommy to him again, although Peter, seemingly relieved for the moment at closing a painful page of his life, would be haunted by the memory of his dog Tommy long beyond his out-of-body experience.

When you fell, Peter, at any time during the fall or when you —landed . . . did you feel any physical pain?

"At the moment of black, no, I didn't feel anything. Then I saw the light and I thought, Oh, my God, I'm not dead. No, I didn't feel any pain. It was black for quite a while. . . .

"At the moment of plopping, it was black. No pain, no sensation at all. Then I felt the light and I got a tremendous heat all over my body."

{5}

The Celestial Jury

Our next session was a somber one. It had barely begun when Jahn, the houseboy, interrupted us and called Peter aside privately to show him a can of something that seemed very important. I watched him remove the lid, and Peter took the can in his hands and showed it to Stephy. It was white and powdery.

"I go now. You come?"

"No, Peter. I can't."

She buried her face in her arms and wept quietly. When she recovered, she said, "That's Max."

We waited while Peter sprinkled the ashes of Max under the great spreading spruce tree on their front lawn.

"That is the place he loved the most. Under that tree. He loved it most. Max. I say my little prayer. And for Tommy, too."

Peter, we go back now, to that moment you fell and when you hit the ground and it was all black. . . . What do you remember after that?

"I remember at the moment of plopping, it was black, no sensation at all. Then I saw the light, like a window that opened, and I wanted to go to that window.

"It was not a window. . . . It was a big ray of light, like a searchlight with three sides, and it was so bright that I almost got blind. . . . It lifted me up . . . sucked me into it so fast. . . . Whoosh! I was talking to it, I was talking to the light. . . . I said, Don't go so fast. . . . All the time I was feeling that I am not dead. . . . The darkness has disappeared. . . . But the light in my face is so bright that I have to close my eyes. . . . Then it is blinding me with heat. . . . My body was burning inside and out . . . hotter and hotter. . . . And my body was traveling with such speed . . . fast, fast, faster! I said to my body, 'Don't go so fast! . . . But I have to go a long way. . . . And it went too fast. . . . Now the heat is burning my skin and I can feel the flesh falling off. . . . First my legs, then my arms, then my whole body is gone from the burning. Then it stops.

"It was a strange light. How can I tell you? It was big, powerful, blazing hot, and shaped like a triangle . . . three sides, like a pyramid. . . . It sucked me up and burned away my body and dropped me on the other world. . . . I had lost my body in the traveling. Now I was walking like a feather . . . no weight . . . floating.

"Then I see all the colors, I hear the music, I hear the voices and I see the people. They were blurry, far away like in a dream, but I knew they were people. I knew I was not dead. . . ."

Peter, did you feel, when you arrived, that you still had your old body, or was it a new body? Did you feel any sensation from the burning?

"My only burning sensation was when I was traveling fast in the light. I was feeling it everywhere, like it burned my whole body. But when I arrived, yes, I was in my body but it was different because my other body was burned off from the heat. Now I felt no pain, no burning, no tiredness from traveling. . . . I had a normal body . . . I had legs and I was walking but I was walking light as a feather, not flying but I could go so fast . . . no weight. I lifted my arms up and they were so light. . . . I had lost the weight when my body was gone from the burning. . . . I did one step and it was like five steps. . . . I felt like I could climb a mountain with steps so light as a feather . . . and I didn't feel at all dizzy. . . . I only felt happy and good . . . my breathing so light . . . my body so light."

Would you describe it as a feeling of weightlessness?

"Yes, exactly, weightlessness. Like my body was on springs."

Did you recognize yourself as Peter Hurkos? Did you remember where you had come from?

"No, I didn't ask questions about myself, who I was, I didn't have time. I was floating on clouds. I was looking at all the colors and all the beauty. Sure, I recognized my own body, I was aware that I was me, but I didn't know who me was. I looked at my hands and they were different, so beautiful, white like baby skin. When I fell I was wearing short pants and a shirt, but now I was wearing a long white gown, transparent, like all the other people."

Were you able to talk?

"No, not at first. I open my mouth but I cannot make a sound. Later I could talk to the people, but now I just saw and felt my hands, and then I heard the voices and the music. I was walking across somewhere like an open field, or in the clouds, and the light was still shining, but this was a different light, a soft transparent light that was everywhere all the time. The first thing I thought was, Where am I? Then I knew I was in another world."

Did you have any memory at all of this world down here, Peter? (He had avoided this question the first time.)

"No. No. My mind was locked off. I was not on this planet any more. And I had no memory of this planet, either. None. I didn't even know where I came from. I could not remember my mother or my father or my sister, or my dog Tommy. All gone. Not there any more. And I was so happy. That's why I wanted to stay in that world.

You said your body was different. Did you feel that you had the same mind?

"No! No! No! Not the same mind! If I was in the same mind, why didn't I remember my dog Tommy, and what happened on the bridge?"

STEPHY: *I think what happened was that he lost his other mind and got another one, a new one. Is that right, Peter?*

"Right. Different mind, same body, when I came back. Up there, a different body, too. Different mind altogether."

TESS: *I don't think you could say he lost his other mind up there, just part of it, part of his memory. Because he came back with two minds in the same body. Is that right, Peter?*

"That's for sure. And I would be so happy if the other one would go away. I didn't have two minds in that other world. That's what they gave me at the trial, for my punishment. Leave me alone. Don't ask me any more questions. I don't want to talk about it now."

He abruptly got up from the table, lifted baby Gloria Ann out of her highchair, went into the organ room, and began playing the Brahms "Lullaby."

Stephy smiled. "He plays that for her all the time and he still doesn't know what it is. You don't believe that? Ask him when he comes back."

Tess added, "He never knows what he's playing. Like he never knows what he's painting. It's just where his hands go."

"He's upset tonight about Max," said Stephy.

"Did you know about Tommy?" I asked Stephy.

"No. I didn't even know he had a dog. But after all, he was only eleven years old when that happened. It's strange how it still disturbs him after all those years."

"Do you know anything about this trial he talks about?"

"No more than you do," she said. "Peter doesn't really like to talk about what happened up there. I'm surprised he's said this much."

"He keeps too much boxed up inside himself," added Tess. "But then maybe that's why he's able to concentrate so well when he's working on a case."

Peter returned with Gloria Ann in his arms. He was not only refreshed but almost ebullient after his session at the organ. He deposited Gloria Ann on the table in front of him, played with her for a while, then placed her in the highchair beside him and said, "Come on, we work now."

"Do you know the Brahms 'Lullaby,' Peter?" I asked.

"No, what's that?"

"It's the one you always play for Gloria Ann," Stephy said.

"I play many things," he said.

"It's this one." Stephy hummed it for him.

"Oh, sure. What's the name?" he asked.

"The Brahms 'Lullaby.' "

"It's beautiful, yes? It comes from the music that I heard up there, in the other world. Like a million organs everywhere, and the singing, like in a big choir all over, singing voices everywhere."

"Who taught you to play it?" I asked, purposely.

"Nobody," he snapped. "How many times do I have to tell you I never study music, I don't read music. It comes from that man with the beard up there. The one on the jury. The composer."

"A composer was on the jury?"

"Sure. Composer, painter, mathematician, scientist, big war hero, medical man, healer—" He stopped.

"Hmmm. Who else, Peter?"

"I don't know. How do I know? They don't tell me who they are."

"Then how did you know one was a painter and a composer and so forth?"

"I see through them. I see what they do. I see paint brushes, one man mixing paints; I see a man playing music, organs, violins; I see warrior, machine guns, tanks; I see a man making sculpture. All are people who have died many years before. Very intellectual people. They all have beards and they were all transparent. That's why I see through them."

Wait a minute, Peter. Let's go back a little. You say these were all people who died many years before. When you were with them, did you feel that you were dead, or were you alive?

"Sure I was alive. Are you kidding? But I was not on this planet any more. I was in another world."

Was it the same kind of feeling you had when you were out of your body and watching your operation?

"Out of my body was the same, but I had entirely different feeling when I watched my operation. I saw myself and I get disgusted. When I was standing in the door watching my operation I had no weight, like on the other planet. But the difference is I saw how they treated and handled me, and turned me over and sawed into my hip, and I was disgusted with my own body. I was standing in the door weightless, yes. It was almost the same as what happened in the other world, but not in the same details, not so beautiful."

Now, let's go back just once more to when you fell, and when you first saw that light. Can you describe how you were sucked into it, how it happened? Did you voluntarily go toward the light or reach for it, or did it just lift you up against your will?

"I don't know . . . but I think I made my own decision to go to the light. First I was in darkness, no dog, no nothing. Then when I saw that light I wanted to get to it. That must be when I stood up and started to walk, and took a few steps. I am grabbing for the light. It was like a long pyramid of light. Yes, it did draw me to it, but I also wanted it, so I went walking, stumbling toward it and reaching for it. Because I didn't want to die and I didn't want to be thinking any more about my dog Tommy. That is the reason I am reaching for the light. And then it sucked me up. . . ."

STEPHY: *But I think Peter was chosen to go there because of his own determination and his strong will. That's what made him grab for the light. He didn't want to die and he got himself to the light. He thinks of it here as his punishment but I think he was chosen to have this gift.*

"You're wrong, Stephy. How do you think you know? You were NOT there. I was there!" Peter roared. "Don't you think I know what they said to me? I told them, I'm the most happy person here and this is where I want to stay. But they said no. They punish me and sent me back."

Who is "they," Peter?

"How many times do I have to tell you? The people in the meeting they held about me, the trial. I was like in front of a firing squad."

When did you first see these people? How many were there?

"I told you NINE!" he nearly shouted it. "I told you, nine men, and all had beards."

Yes, we know. But when did you first see them? Did you see other people, too? How did you get to the—meeting place? What did the meeting place look like? Were other people there besides those nine men? Can you describe exactly how or when you first saw them after you arrived on that other planet?

"Sure, I can describe it for you. I will even draw you a picture of the meeting hall. Tess, bring me my drawing pad. It was a big round dome, bright white, with the light shining on it, part open, like a shell. . . ."

STEPHY: *Like the Hollywood Bowl?*

"No, no, no, Stephy. Be quiet. Now listen to me. . . . I'll describe to you what happened from the beginning, when I arrived. I told you I am walking like on a feather and I hear the music and the voices singing, right? I see people, too, but they are only faces and far away in the distance. They look like small people, all smiling, all singing, like a choir. But I don't see them close up yet, only the faces, and there is a film over them, like gauze.

"Then I see these figures coming toward me, tall figures all in white. They are all pointing at me and when they come closer I see they are not smiling. They are still pointing and I know something is wrong. They come closer and I see now they all have beards. . . . I do not know where they come from. . . . Maybe out of the clouds. . . . They seem to be floating toward me, walking like on feathers, and they all have their arms out in front of them, pointing at me, like wanting me to go away. "I thought, what have I done? And then I heard them saying, like all together in one voice, 'You don't belong here, you don't belong here, you don't belong here! What are you doing here? You are not ready to die.' . . . And I could hear the voices in the choirs behind them in the distance, louder and louder—'You don't belong here, you don't belong here . . . you don't belong . . .'

"Then the figures seemed to be whispering between themselves, and I knew they were having a discussion about me. They did not look angry but they looked very solemn. They said to me, 'Come. . . .' And they led me into the meeting hall under the big white dome. . . .

"There was a long white marble table and nine white marble chairs in a straight row. . . . They all walked behind the table and sat down in the chairs, and I stood in front of them, facing them, looking up at them. The table was on a raised platform, high, like a judge's bench in a courtroom, only this was a long white marble table with the nine men. . . . Behind them, in the middle, was another platform, higher, and on this platform there was another big marble chair, but more important . . . more like a throne, only built in the shape of a human being, a person, especially the legs. . . . It was empty, always empty both times I was there. . . .

"They had another discussion about me between each other, and then they told me, 'You do not belong here. Your time is not here yet. Your work is not finished. But we have to decide what to do with you. And we will have to talk to the Master about this. We will permit you to stay until we talk to the Master. Then we give you our decision.'

Peter reached for his drawing pad and quickly drew for us the whole scene, the domed meeting hall, the table and chairs where the bearded figures were seated, and the empty throne-chair.

Then he slammed the drawing pad on the table, stood up and stretched, and said, "I have to rest now. I have a murder case at midnight."

{6}

Out of Body

THIS SEEMS AN APPROPRIATE PLACE, BEFORE PROCEEDING WITH Peter's out-of-body odyssey, to interpose some background notes on so-called out-of-body experiences for readers who may not be aware of their authenticity, as well as for Peter, who has never read any of the literature on psychic phenomena and who is totally unaware of the significance of an out-of-body experience or the current interest and research in this area.

I cannot vouch for what Peter saw, felt, or experienced in that "other world." He was there. We were not, as he so often reminded us.

I am merely reporting it as he told it.

Although his detailed version of what he encountered in that other world may be unique, the actual out-of-body experience is not. Many have had similar experiences.

The out-of-body phenomenon has fascinated and bewildered philosophers and scientists for centuries. The experience is usually the same in that the individuals to whom it happens suddenly discover that they have left their bodies.

Sometimes they seem to be floating above or away from their bodies. Sometimes they may just find themselves standing and looking at their own bodies lying on a bed, as Peter did during his operation. Or sometimes they visit places unknown to them, as Peter did on his four-day journey to another planet.

Skeptics may disbelieve, yet these out-of-body experiences have happened and continue to happen. Thousands of case histories have been recorded in books, articles, and medical or psychiatric journals. The experience usually occurs under stress or during times of crisis—illness, a close brush with death, anesthesia, an operation. It occurs spontaneously and without the conscious will of the person who experiences it. As a spontaneous phenomenon it cannot be subjected to scientific scrutiny and must depend entirely on the individual's testimony for verification. Nevertheless, it has been the subject of serious study by some highly reputable doctors and scientists.

Dr. Russell Noyes, an associate professor of psychiatry at the University of Iowa College of Medicine, has made a study of the out-of-body or "transcendental" experiences of many who have had almost fatal encounters with sudden death. He has discovered that their recollections follow a distinct, almost predictable, pattern.

This pattern can be broken down into three chronological divisions: *resistance, review,* and *transcendence.* (Italics mine.)

In the first stage, Dr. Noyes explains, the victim's realization that death is imminent precipitates a violent struggle to gain control of the situation so that he can remain alive.

This describes precisely Peter's feeling when he fell from his painter's ladder. His first thoughts were, I don't want to die! I don't want to die.

If the danger is not overcome, the victim often surrenders to a feeling of passive resignation, which in turn leads to a sensation of profound tranquility. And at this point, Dr. Noyes says, the person may experience a peculiar split between body and mind—a state that apparently permits him to "watch" his own death with a feeling of detachment—just as Peter "watched" his own operation, as well as his almost fatal encounter with sudden death during his fall. At the same time, according to Dr. Noyes, the victim enters the "review" stage, and he often sees what seems to be his past life laid out before him. Vivid memories, usually of a pleasant nature, flash through his mind in rapid succession, somewhat like a speeded-up movie, says Dr. Noyes of the case histories he has studied.

In Peter's review stage during his fall, certain events of his past life flashed by vividly in rapid succession like a speeded-up movie —but they were not of a pleasant nature.

They were dominated by the one unhappiest event of his life, the drowning of his dog, Tommy, which had occurred some twenty years before his near fatal fall.

Dr. Noyes says that a third of the cases he studied claimed to have experienced the review stage but a smaller number, only 25 per cent—those who came still closer to death—entered the third stage, transcendence. In this final phase, he says, the person sometimes feels as though he has slipped beyond the restrictive boundaries of past and future.

"It was the most perfect state of easeful joy that I ever experienced," said one of his case histories—a young poet who came close to death through drowning. "There was no sadness or sickness from which I wished to escape." These were Peter's words also: "No sadness or sickness or sorrow. . . ."

A Swiss geology professor who had a close brush with death in a sixty-six-foot fall from a mountain peak described it this way:

"Everything was transfigured, as though by a heavenly light, and everything was beautiful without grief, without anxiety and pain. . . . I became ever more surrounded by a splendid blue heaven with delicate roseate and violet cloudlets."

If Peter knew the words, that is the way he would say it. . . .

Typical descriptions of this last stage of transcendence, says Dr. Noyes, include flashes of light, visions, ecstasy, the presence of an "outside force" and, in a few instances, a sense of "fusion with nature." And, he adds, most victims recall at least an altered mental state in which time slows down and perceptions seem more acute than usual.

There can be no doubt that Peter Hurkos experienced what Dr. Noyes calls the third stage and final phase—transcendence—or what others call an out-of-body experience.

While Peter was in his stage of transcendence, his feeling, as he describes it, was one of being alive and aware, although his experiences had a dreamlike quality as if seen through a veil.

But he also insists that he was dead, that he had died and was "reborn." I tried to clarify this.

"What the hell, my parents and all my friends told me I had died and was reborn. They said this is not the same Peter any more."

"But did *you* think you were dead?"

"Yes. Absolutely."

"Do you, Peter Hurkos, sitting here at this table right now, really think that you were dead for four days?"

"Oh, no, no. Up there in that other world I was alive. But down here on this planet, I was dead."

"For how long?" I asked.

"How do I know? There is no time. When I was dead I was in the darkness. And then I go from the darkness to the light."

Medical authorities acknowledge that the precise moment of death is extremely difficult to determine. And all of us have read reports of actual cases in which a doctor has pronounced a patient dead—sometimes an infant, sometimes an adult—and then signs of life reappear. Such cases are rare, but they do exist.

Whether Peter ever was actually dead, even if for only a few seconds or minutes, we will probably never know.

But if we accept the premise that there are varied phenomena of *being* in that state *between* life and death, then Peter's out-of-body experiences must confirm that we do indeed exist in more dimensions than we realize.

A New York man, Victor D. Solow, vividly described his own experience with that "other reality" beyond in a *Reader's Digest* "First Person" Award story titled "I Died at 10:52 A.M.," published in October 1974.

Mr. Solow had gone for a ten-minute jog with his wife when he suffered a heart attack. For twenty-three minutes, his heart stopped, and with it all signs of life.

Excerpts from his story may help shed light on Peter's experience:

"Sometime later I was aware that my eyes were open. But I was still part of another world. It seemed that by chance I had been given this human body and it was difficult to wear."

He told his doctor, "I feel like I've been there and I've come back."

The doctor's response was, "It's true. You were there and now you are back."

. . . *A hard time followed. I could not connect with the world around me. Was I really here now, or was it an illusion? Was that other condition of being I had just experienced the reality, or was that the illusion? I would lie there and observe my body with suspicion and amazement. It seemed to be doing things of its own volition and I was a visitor within. How strange to see my hand reach out for something. Eating, drinking, watching people had a dreamlike, slow-motion quality as if seen through a veil.*

During those first few days I was two people. My absent-mindedness and strange detachment gave the doctors pause. Perhaps the brain had been damaged after all. Their concern is reflected in hospital records. "Retrograde amnesia and difficulty with subsequent current events was recognized. . . ."

. . . Family, friends began to ask (after his recovery) what "death was like." *Could I remember what had happened during those twenty-three minutes when heart and breathing stopped? I found that the experience could not easily be communicated.*

Later, feeling and thinking my way back into the experience, I

*discovered why I could not make it a simple recital of events:
when I left my body I also left all sensory human tools behind
with which to perceive the world we take for real. But I found
that I now* knew *certain things about my place in this our world
and my relationship to that other reality. My knowing was not
through my brain but with another part of me which I cannot explain.*

*For me, the moment of transition from life to death—what else
can one call it?—was easy. There was no time for fear, pain or
thought. There was no chance "to see my whole life before me,"
as others have related. The last impression I can recall lasted a
brief instant. I was moving at high speed toward a net of great
luminosity.* [Precisely like Peter.] *. . . For a brief moment my
speed appeared to slow down. Then I was in the grid. The instant
I made contact with it, the vibrant luminosity increased to a
blinding intensity which drained, absorbed and transformed me at
the same time. There was no pain. The sensation was neither
pleasant nor unpleasant but completely consuming. The nature of
everything had changed. . . .*

*The grid was like a transformer, and energy converter transport-
ing me through form and into formlessness, beyond time and
space. Now I was not in a place, nor even a dimension, but rather
in a condition of being. This new "I" was not the I which I knew,
but rather a distilled essence of it, yet something vaguely familiar. . . .*

*. . . These experiences outside the dimensions of our known re-
ality did not "happen" as if I were on some sort of voyage I could
recollect. Rather, I discovered them afterward, rooted in my consciousness as a kind of unquestionable knowing. Being of a somewhat skeptical turn of mind, I am willing to grant the possibility
that this is a leftover of some subtle form of brain damage. I
know, however, that since my return from that other condition of
being, many of my attitudes toward our world have changed and
continue to change, almost by themselves. A recurrent nostalgia
remains for that other reality, that condition of indescribable
stillness and quiet where the "I" is a part of a harmonious
whole. . . .*

*I am glad I am here and now. But I know this marvelous place
. . . is only one of many realities through which I must travel to
distant and unknown destinations.*

For centuries men have preoccupied themselves with trying to
unravel the mysteries of death. Psychics, seers, clairvoyants, ancient philosophers and religious mystics, modern psychologists,
parapsychologists, and even some medical brain researchers,
neurologists, and other scientists have pursued the subject with
great fervor—but few conclusions.

Most agree, however, that the out-of-body phenomenon is an
actuality. Many accept it as proof of "life after death" or at least
the existence of a "soul," a separate entity independent of the
body. Some have claimed that it is possible to separate the "astral
body" from the physical body at will—and even go traveling in it!
This is called "astral travel."

Having had no experience in this cosmic realm, I would not
wish to tangle here with the metaphysicians. But it is my opinion
that Peter's other-world experience had nothing to do with so-
called astral travel, which is a strictly metaphysical concept.

Rather it had to do with the genuine out-of-body phenomena,
which many have experienced, as has been well documented.

The "other body" has been called by many names: the "subtle
body," the "astral body," the "etheric body," the "ethereal body,"
the "fluidic body," the "second body," the "double body," the
"soul," the "mind," the "psyche," the "spiritual essence," and so
on and on.

Whatever it is, there appears to be some general agreement
that man is more than just a physiological organism.

Even Dr. Wilder Penfield of McGill University in Montreal,
one of the greatest of all neurophysiologists and known as the father of modern neurophysiology, has conceded that the human
brain is something more than a physical mechanism.

Dr. Penfield has performed numerous operations in which he
has removed massive segments of a patient's brain. Still the
"mind" seemed to carry on as before without any disturbance of

consciousness, he says. "Perhaps we will always be forced to visualize a spiritual element . . . a spiritual essence that is capable of controlling the mechanism. The machine will never fully explain man, nor mechanisms the nature of the spirit."

Dr. Carl Jung, the psychiatrist, once wrote of hearing the "voice of *my second personality*" (italics mine), and spoke of the "powers slumbering in the psyche, of which we are seldom aware. . . . We are a psychic process which we do not control, or only partly direct. . . ."

Camille Flammarion, the distinguished French astronomer and thinker (1842–1925), whose trilogy on *Death and Its Mystery* (*Before Death, At the Moment of Death, After Death*) was regarded as one of his greatest achievements, declared, "Every man and even every animal has a double, a fluid body. This truth is recognizable by virtue of the fact that those who have had parts of the body amputated feel pain at the extremities of the limbs which they no longer have." (Doctors explain this away as wish-fulfilling hallucinations, or as nerves still registering what is gone.) Flammarion described the double body as being "an invisible active aura about our bodies."

On a more up-to-date note, however, Soviet scientists say this "invisible" aura is no longer invisible. They claim to have made it possible for everyone to see at least part of the aura through their highly touted process of Kirlian photography. Sheila Ostrander and Lynn Schroeder, in their book *Psychic Discoveries Behind the Iron Curtain* (Prentice-Hall, 1970), wrote, "The Soviets have many times photographed the moment of death. . . . Little by little as a plant's or animal's physical body dies, Russians saw sparks and flares of the bioplasmic body shooting out into space, swimming away and disappearing from sight. Gradually there was no luminescence at all coming from the dead plant or animal. . . ."

This proves, it is claimed, that "we have not one, but two bodies."

The Russians call the other one the "bioplasmic body."

Personally, I would be more inclined to lean toward the astrological explanation for Peter's double body, double mind, or double whatever it is. He was born a double Gemini, on the cusp, May 21, 1911, at five o'clock in the morning. Gemini, as any astrology buff knows, is the sign of the Twins, and the most psychic of all the zodiacal signs. Should not a double Gemini, therefore, give him not only a double psyche but quadruple?

And a numerologist could undoubtedly provide even a more mystical reason for those *nine* men on that celestial jury who told him he didn't belong up there.

Deep within my own psyche was a persistent twinge of premonition that Peter's other self lay buried somewhere between his painting "Mur Woods" and the locked-up mystery of Ana Kaneel, the Indonesian nurse from the Zuidwal. She must have known him while he was out of his body. Why did he not want to see her?

{7}

The Other World

THERE WERE A MILLION QUESTIONS WE WERE ANXIOUS TO ASK PETER. But the first one I asked at our next session was, "Did you see any children in that other world?"

"Sure, many children," he said.

"Did you happen to see that little boy with the black curly hair? The one you painted with his face in the clouds?"

"No! No! NO! You don't listen to what I say! He is the man with the beard as a child. I only see those jurymen when they are old and dead and have beards. How do I know what they looked like when they were children?"

"Then how do you know the little boy you painted is one of those men as a child?"

"I just know. Don't ask me to explain, I just know. That's

where my hands went . . . the boy and the man with the beard in the same picture, so it's the same person, don't you see? How else can you explain it?"

Once Peter gets something fixed in his head, he won't budge from it, and he becomes irritated, sometimes belligerent, if he thinks you doubt him.

"Do you know which of those nine men on the jury is the one you painted?"

"No. They all look the same. Same face, same voice, same beard, same eyes, all staring at me. . . . All famous people from history. . . . All have high education . . . and I was standing there a dumb man . . . no education. I was frightened."

How did you know they were famous people, Peter?

"I tell you I saw through them. They didn't tell me what they were. One was a man who wrote about the future. I saw a big pile of books through him, the war hero I saw war machinery, the composer I saw music and notes. . . . I never knew their names. I only knew what they did in this world down here because I saw it."

You mentioned a chemist. What did you see him doing?

"I saw bubbles and bottles and boiling. I saw things all around him."

What did you see behind the mathematician?

"What do you mean—mathematician?" Peter asked blankly.

You told us the last time that one of the men up there at the jury table was a mathematician.

"What is mathematician?" he asked again.

He had definitely mentioned a mathematician in the previous session. It seemed incredible that he would not know what a mathematician is, but between his simplicity of mind, his language barrier, and his psychic grasp of things unknown to him, he often gets his words and thoughts mixed up. With these handicaps, the wonder is that he does as well as he does.

We explained to him what a mathematician is, and he said, "Oh yes. Man working with meters. . . . Fittings and numbers and drawings, like what you call blueprint type things. . . ."

Do you remember any of the designs from the blueprints?
"No. Only they were more underwater things. Like a kind of submarine. . . . All under water. And then I saw the numbers and symbols and drawings from when they are building the pyramids."
Did you see someone building the pryamids?
"No. Not there at the jury table. But later the man with the beard took me through them, showed me how they're built. He was like my guide, took me around and showed me everything, the mountains, craters, how the people live. . . ."
Do you know which one of the nine men was your guide—the composer, the artist—who?
"Always different—never the same. They all look the same yes, but they only speak to me one at a time. After the first meeting they all left but sometimes they come back to me, talk to me, then they go away. . . . But never more than one at a time. . . . Never together. . . . Only together when they take me to trial. I did not see them much in between. I don't know where they lived. Not in the houses I saw where other people live. Maybe they live on another planet, just come here for my trial, to punish me. . . ."
What kind of language did they speak?
"Many different languages . . . or by telepathy . . . I don't know . . . I only remember what they said. But I remember every word."
Was there any one of the men at the jury table who spoke to you first, or who impressed you the most?
"Yes, definitely. He was the one on the end, at the left. He talked to me first, and he was staring at me, more than the others. I remember the eyes. He asked me questions but when I answered, he couldn't hear me. I was yelling, and he was staring straight through me. I think he was psychic, or reading my lips. . . . I did not know what 'psychic' was then, but now I think he must have been. When I saw through his body, I saw music notes and an organ."
Can you identify the man, Peter?

"No. How can I? He never told me his name. Don't ask me again. I already told you. I have to rest now."

When Peter came back from his rest he was again refreshed and ready to tell us about the other people, aside from the nine wise men, he saw in his other world.

"When I came out of the meeting I saw many people around me, all transparent. . . . They were little people, all like small children with soft round faces like an apple. . . . And there were beautiful flowers and fruit and trees. . . . The ground was so soft, it was like walking on a balloon. . . . And colors that I cannot describe, I cannot bring on canvas. . . . Orange and purple and crimson above, and blue down below. . . . But the people, their hair and faces were all the same. No black, brown, yellow or anything . . . all white, transparent . . . but all in pale colors from the light . . . the reflection of that light from a distance. . . .

"Then I saw their *cupoles* where they live. . . . And I saw all the little people coming out, and they welcomed me as though they expected me. I asked, 'What are these? They are so beautiful.' And they said, these are our *cupoles*. It was what they lived in, the *cupoles*. . . ."

Peter pronounced the word like koo-poles. Did he mean cupola, a small dome on a roof? No. Definitely not. He seemed to know what a cupola was. Was his word cupoles a Dutch word? No, he said, it was not a Dutch word, it was the word he heard only up there to describe the houses the little people lived in.

"The people told me that's what their houses were called—koo-poles. Here, I draw you a picture."

He took his drawing pad and sketched pictures of the *cupoles*— or koo-poles—where the "little people" lived, and they were indeed like cupolas: small, domed, round dwellings. "They were like igloos," Peter said. "No doors or windows . . . I went in and out of many of them. They were all flat and round inside, not square, never in a corner shape. . . . Everything was round, like half an egg, or a half shell. . . . And on the outside they were all shiny blue, orange, yellow, purple, all different reflections from the light. . . ."

From the way Peter described it, there were apparently no appurtenances from this earth, no bathrooms, bedrooms, kitchens, no telephone or electrical wires outside, no automobiles, airplanes, monorails, or means of transportation—except iridescent half shells, in which the little people sometimes just sat and sometimes rode to and fro, wherever they wanted to go.

Were they like flying objects?

"No, no, no! I have seen flying objects but they are from a different planet. Not where I was."

How old were these people?

"You couldn't see the difference between old and young. . . . They don't have an answer for age. . . . Same as there was no difference between night and day. . . . It gets dark at night, yes, but it is not the same darkness. There is always the soft light, a pyramid of light shining down on the *cupoles*, even when I was walking at night. Like three angles shining from the top of the mountains, and lighting up the whole place like a football field. . . . It is the light which makes the colors like in a rainbow, but more transparent. . . ."

What language did you speak with these people?

"I talked in Dutch but no difference. They knew it and understood it, any language you use. A lot of them talked by telepathy. . . . And there was so much peace and quiet and happiness, it was unbelievable. . . ."

What kind of food did they eat?

"All the food they ate was round, that's all I remember. Beautiful fruit from the trees. . . . They didn't need much food there. And there were fields of flowers, tall and round, like sunflowers, and lots of seeds on the ground. . . ."

Did you ever wonder where you were? Did you ever ask the little people or those men with the beards where you were, what other world you were in?

"No, I remember thinking when I first arrived, I was so confused, and I asked myself, Where am I? But then I did not ask any of the people I met because I was too happy to be there. I wanted to stay. . . .''

When did you first meet one of those men again—the men from the jury table, the ones who acted as your guides?

"The first one was the man with the beard who took me to the well. But I don't know which one he was. He came up to me and he said, 'You have to go in the water and prepare yourself. I see you have breathing trouble. In your world you have two lungs. In ours we have only one lung.'

"I asked how could he breathe with only one lung, and he said, 'I'll show you.'

"He was dressed all in white, and he didn't take off his white clothing but I could see through it. It was transparent. I could see there was only one lung. . . . I looked at the other little people around me and I could see they had only one lung.

"The man with the beard said, 'Come, we have to take you to the well.' And he led me to the bathtub, but it was not a bathtub . . . it was round like a half shell that carries water, oily and soft. And he said, 'If you go in there you will breathe easier. . . . You will learn how to use only one lung. . . . So I went in the water. I was embarrassed with everyone looking at me, but when I came out I was happy. . . . I could breathe fresh air now, I was breathing out of one lung. In that world the air was thin, so you didn't need to use that much oxygen. . . .

"Then he took me out to the mountains and the rocks, and there was this light coming out from the rocks. . . . I asked, 'How does the light come out from the rocks?' And he said, 'We do this with water, like a saw. The water cuts the rock in three angles. These light up when it starts to get dark at night.'

"It was the energy in the rocks that was the light. It comes from the mountains. . . . There were three angles on the bottom but no light at all there, the light was on the top.''

Was this like the light you saw after you fell, Peter?

"Yes, that is the same light I saw before, the light when I came out of the darkness. My eye was always following that light. But when I arrived there, in that other world, the light had stopped its burning. . . . It was like . . . whoosh! . . . all burned out . . .

and now it was just soft light with colors shining everywhere, around all the people and the cupoles and all over. . . . Even in the water. . . . First I heard the water, then I saw it, like a crater . . . but clear water and no wind . . . and you could see the bottom like colors in the rainbow. . . . I don't know if that's what they drink from, I don't know. . . . I tell you only what I see for sure. . . ."

We asked Peter to explain further how they cut the rocks with water.

"First," he said, "they can pick up a five- or eight-ton rock like a spoon. So I said, 'How do you do this?' He said, 'We have to sprinkle this with the fluid to make it weightless.' And he showed me how they use the water what comes out of the mountains, and you wet the big rocks and then you cut the rocks with water. . . . When the rock is wet it gets light, it has no weight. And when the water dries off, there is weight again.

"I tried to lift a rock and I couldn't, so he showed me. He took a bucket, like this . . . not the ones we have here, but a round bucket, like half an egg shell . . . and he filled it with water and got the water he needed over the rock. Then it became very light, and with the weightlessness we could pick it up. . . . Then when it was dried up, it was the same heavy rock, solid. . . ."

But what did you mean when you said they cut the rocks with water?

"He showed me that, too. The cutting was not done by measurement. He had a long stick and it was filled with water which sprinkled out at one end. He made a straight line with the water, and he went back and forth, soaking it. . . . This is how they cut the rocks. . . . It was a fluid, but not oil and not really water. . . . And when it sprinkled out and made the straight line, the rock was cut when it was completely wet. . . . Then he lift it up and it was two pieces. . . ."

What else do you remember from that other world?

"Many things. I tell you. But everything was clean . . . no dirt or dust. . . . And the skies were almost every time the same, but not exactly blue like we see it. More transparent, with many colors. . . . Everyone smiling and happy. No illness, no hospitals, no schools, nothing from this planet."

Did you see anyone you recognized . . . your grandparents, relatives, friends who had died?

"No. Nobody."

This guide, or these guides, that you had—did any of them ever tell you who they were?

"No, never. I told you that."

But didn't they give you a hint of what they did down here on this planet before they died?

"Yes. One told me he was a healer, and I would have the same gift. And the other one, the music man, the composer, told me he did not finish his work, and I did not finish my work, and I have to go back and finish. . . . You will have a gift. . . . And one told me I would use my gift to work with police. I said, 'What do you mean? I don't like police. I was only a house painter. But I don't want a gift. I want to stay here.' . . . When he talked to me it was like more than one person . . . sometimes it was one man and sometimes it was another. . . . He was always like a double person too."

{8}

The Composer

I DECIDED IT WAS TIME TO TEST ONE OF THE PSYCHIC GIFTS PETER had brought back with him. He always works best, receives his strongest "vibrations" and insight, when he is touching an object. This is called "psychometry."

When working criminal cases he insists on having something very personal from the victim—to "psychometrize"—a piece of clothing, preferably underclothing, or a lock of hair, or, as in one case recently, the fingernails from a dead girl's body!

Whenever possible he sleeps with the objects, after which he can usually provide answers and clues with astonishing accuracy— just as the great psychic Edgar Cayce as a child could learn his school lessons by sleeping with his textbooks and later was able to diagnose illnesses and predict the future from the visions that came to him while sleeping.

Peter is not 100 per cent accurate and has never claimed to be. Such claims are for charlatans. And he vehemently denies that he makes "predictions." He doesn't like that word and does not wish to be known as a seer. Nevertheless, as many will attest, he frequently has had psychic flashes or foreknowledge of certain events. The parapsychologists call this "precognition."

But Peter's psychic skills seem to lean more toward retrocognition—looking into the past through psychometry.

He once worked on a murder case in Virginia with Dr. F. Regis Riesenman, a well-known Washington, D.C., psychiatrist and criminologist. (This is related in detail in my book *The Psychic World of Peter Hurkos.*) When I asked Dr. Riesenman how he would compare Peter Hurkos with Edgar Cayce, he replied without hesitation:

"Edgar Cayce was the greatest psychic who ever lived. He was able to transcend time and space and communicate with a universal subconscious mind to treat the ill and predict the future. . . . Peter Hurkos, on the other hand, is the greatest psychic who ever lived with the gift of retrocognition. That means regressing, seeing into the past, going back in time for his psychic knowledge. Yes, he also has the gift of precognition, foretelling the future, but not to the extent that Edgar Cayce had it.

"Peter's real gift is retrocognition, going backward in time for spontaneous readings on people, and his best work is done on criminal cases. I say he's the greatest psychic who ever lived in this field—reading people both spontaneously and on demand in criminal cases, especially murders and missing people. . . . Give him a scrap of clothing or a wisp of hair," he said, "and he might be able to tell you everything a man has done or is planning to do."

For our project at the moment it was impossible to obtain a scrap of clothing or a wisp of hair, but I was sure that pictures, photographs, would work just as well for our purpose.

Over the years I have watched Peter psychometrize literally thousands of pictures, photographs, maps, and sealed envelopes, as well as many other objects, and his percentage of accuracy usually has been high enough to whet my curiosity, if not totally convince my perversely skeptical mind.

Stephy and Tess carried in an armload each of thick, heavy, big blue-bound books and stacked them on one end of the table. They were the complete, six-volume set of Grove's Dictionary of Music and Musicians, with biographies and photographs of all the great composers of the past.

Stephy had borrowed them from her friend Kathryn Grayson, a veteran star of those great Metro-Goldwyn-Mayer musicals, still a star on the concert circuit, an accomplished musician and light-opera singer.

Kathryn had heard Peter play many times, at her home and his. She had recognized in his music certain strains predominantly from Puccini, Tschaikovsky, and Schubert, as well as countless Italian folk songs.

"But he plays them only in bits and pieces," she told us. "It's as though he is remembering them from somewhere and then he goes off completely into another world with his own music that no one ever heard before. He has such a great feeling for music, it's too bad he has never studied, never learned to read music or to play a composition clear through to the end. But then it's hard to harness someone like Peter," she said.

Well, we were going to try to harness him long enough to psychometrize the photographs of the composers and see if he could identify the one he saw—up there. It was a long shot, but worth a try. By now we had acquired the habit of referring to his other world as simply "up there."

Peter, we're going back into time now, way back, even long before your fall. We're going to show you pictures of people who lived and died a long time ago, even before you were born.

He interrupted, "I don't know anything about them. I only know the ones I saw up there."

All right, you said one of the men was a composer. You saw and heard music all around him.

"That's right. He asked me what impressed me most up there,

and I said, 'Your beautiful music.' But I was dumb. I did not know what music it was. . . .'"

We began opening the pages and pushing the books in front of him, one by one. We started with Puccini, Tschaikovsky, and Schubert because Kathryn Grayson had told us that they were the ones whose music he played most.

He only touched them lightly and pushed them aside. "No. No. Not this one. No. He doesn't have a beard. No, definitely not this one. The composer I saw there had a mustache and the beard."

This was the first time he had mentioned a mustache, but I decided to pass on that one. We had enough problems trying to cope with one beard—or non-beard—at a time.

I could see that he wasn't really interested in psychometrizing a photograph unless the man had a beard. For skeptics who might question such an unscientific and elementary "test" and say that Peter recognized the composers by their photographs or their names printed in small type below, I hasten to say, Hogwash! Let those who doubt disprove it. Certainly Peter was looking at reproductions of actual photographs instead of "seeing" them through sealed envelopes as he can do very well. And certainly he could have read the name below the picture if we had not covered it up, although he doesn't read all that well.

Even if he had read the name and recognized the picture as one he had seen before, he would not have associated the two. His knowledge in this area was minimal. He didn't know Mozart from Mendelssohn, either from their photographs or their music.

When we put Mozart's picture in front of him, he touched it and said, "This man here, he died young. [I didn't know it until I looked it up; Mozart was thirty-five when he died.] He started his music when he was a child."

"Do you know who this man is?" I asked Peter.

"No."

"This is Mozart. Have you ever heard about Mozart?"

"Yes, I heard about him. He was a composer."

"Do you know that he was a child prodigy, a boy genius?"

"No. I didn't know that. But I didn't see him at the trial. Maybe I heard some of his music, I don't know."

"How about this one? [Chopin] . . ."

"No, no."

"This one . . . ?"

"No. Not this one. His eyes are not strong enough. And his music is too heavy." It was Wagner.

We next showed him a picture of Bach. He closed his eyes and slowly ran his fingertips over the picture.

"Yes, could be this one up at the trial. But he wrote heavy, heavy music. . . . A lonely man, locked up in his room for days . . . and he was drinking when he was playing heavy music. . . . I don't like his music."

"Do you know his name, Peter?"

"No."

"That's Bach, one of the fathers of music."

"Maybe that's who he was but I don't like his music. Too heavy."

Stephy said, "But you are always playing the Bach-Gounod 'Ave Maria,' Peter. That's what Kathryn says it is."

"Oh, yes?" Peter asked in a tone of surprise. "If I hear it up there, then I play it. I don't like the music from this man, but could be he's the one up there at the trial. Could be."

We then showed him a picture of Brahms—with a beard.

He barely touched it and said, "Yes, I think this is the one. They all had beards."

"That's Brahms," I said. "Remember you play the Brahms 'Lullaby' for Gloria Ann?"

"I don't know it," he said.

"Yes, you do, Peter," said Stephy. She hummed it for him again.

"Oh, yes, I do know it. But I didn't know that's what it's called because the people up there didn't say who they were. But maybe I hear some of their music there."

"Do you think this is the composer you saw up there—on the jury?"

"Could be, yes. I'm not sure."

He kept both Brahms and Bach in front of him and continued to rub his fingers across them, sometimes with his eyes closed.

"Maybe both," he mumbled.

Stephy and I took the book from him and turned the pages to

another picture. We looked at each other, shrugged, and hesitated. The man had a fairly young face with flowing hair but not a trace of a mustache or beard. We knew it would be useless to show this one to Peter. But we pushed it in front of him anyway. Why not?

To our amazement, Peter took one look at the picture and began pounding his index finger on it, shouting with excitement, "That's him! That's the one! Definite! Definite! It's the eyes, the eyes, same eyes that stare through me more than the others. . . ."

"But Peter . . . he doesn't have a beard."

"Oh, yes, he does. . . . He did up there. . . . Don't you know when you die, your hair grows, takes last bit of juice from your body . . . ?" He jumped up from his chair in excitement, stretched his long arms toward the picture, tapping it with both hands in a frenzy. "I tell you he is the one. No beard here in this world but I recognize the eyes. Yes! Yes! Yes! I hear the music . . . dramatic music . . . sometimes heavy and sometimes sweet. . . . Lots of piano, organ, violins, and cello, too. All the music I heard in the other world is this person. But he didn't finish his music. He told me. . . ."

Stephy reached for the phone and called Kathryn Grayson. "Did you ever hear Peter play any Beethoven?" she asked.

Kathryn said no, never. But Beethoven played music from other composers as well as his own, she told Stephy.

Peter sat down and quietly stared at the picture. It was a photo reproduction of the famous J. C. Stieler painting of Beethoven. He took a sheet of paper and placed it under the eyes, covering the rest of the face. The words tumbled out of him: "Yes, yes. The eyes. . . . Definite. . . ." He moved the sheet of paper slowly down the face, saying, "Same nose, too, same mouth, same chin. . . . But the eyes tell me this is the one I met. . . ."

What else did his eyes tell you, Peter?

Peter's own eyes now took on that glazed, staring, semitrance look that comes over him when he is possessed by his other body. He pushed the book aside. He wasn't even looking at the picture of Beethoven, nor at us, as he began to talk.

He seemed to retreat moodily inside himself and sat as though listening to something with an inner ear, seeing something with a third eye, and feeling something with profound emotion and sorrow. Even later, as I listened incredulously to the tapes, I was still moved by the deep, halting words that came out. They were the words of a man almost unbearably tortured by something he had experienced somewhere before, either in this life or another.

Peter started, falteringly, "This man said, 'I was on your earth, in your world, but I didn't get to finish the work I had to do because they needed me here.' Then he told me that I was not finished with my work down here, and I would have to go back. 'But I love your music here,' I told him, and I started to cry. Tears. . . . His eyes were always staring right through me, and then he said I would go back with a gift from him. He was a very kind man. This was the person who gave me the inspiration for my music. . . ."

Do you know anything else about him, what he did in this life, Peter?

"Yes, he played the organ and piano. . . . Very emotional man, sometimes very strange, very sensitive, strong temper but also strong intellect and sometimes deep melancholy. . . ." Peter was still in a daze: "I see a disease. Coughing and blood. Tears, tears, two hours sleep and the resistance down, like TB but he didn't die of TB. . . . Spitting of blood. . . . Very sick man. . . . Unhappy he didn't finish the end of his music. He had a big tragedy. Something wrong."

Neither Stephy, Tess, nor I knew anything about Beethoven's personal life, except that he was deaf. Peter did not mention this specifically, but his repeated reference to the "eyes staring right through me," the allusion to his tragedy, and his previous comment that "it was like he couldn't hear me and he was reading my lips" would seem to indicate that Peter had tuned in to his deafness.

Stephy began reading excerpts from Beethoven's biography.

"Look, it says here he was not only a composer, he was also an organist and pianist at the court of the emperor's brother in Vienna. . . . He was a very emotional, demonstrative man. He would stop in the middle of a performance if he didn't like the way people were acting. He would just get up and quit," Stephy said, paraphrasing. "Peter is like that. If he doesn't like the vibrations, he just walks out. . . . Listen to this . . . about the 'abruptness of his manners . . . [reading] his sensitiveness was extreme, his temper ungovernable and his mode of expression often quite unjustifiable.' That sounds like Peter sometimes. . . . Sometimes he [Beethoven] was in 'deepest melancholy.' . . . His health was bad . . . lots of diseases . . . syphilitic, chronic liver trouble, and during an illness later in life, they bled him several times . . . he was always going to doctors . . . and he did leave an unfinished symphony, the Tenth Symphony, it says here, but he had it all sketched out in his head. . . . And he wrote illegibly. Look at this [pointing to Beethoven's signature], but Peter's is even worse," Stephy said.

She continued reading:

" '. . . He had the breadth of jaw which distinguishes so many men of great intellect; the mouth firm and determined, the lips protruded with a look almost of fierceness: but his eyes were the special feature of the face, and it was from them that the earnestness and sincerity of his character beamed forth. . . . When under the influence of inspiration, they dilated in a peculiar way. His head was large, the forehead both high and broad, and the hair abundant. It was originally black, but the last years of his life, though as thick as ever, became quite white. . . .' "

Stephy stopped and cried out, "Listen to this! 'Beard or mustache he never wore. If he had done so his beard would have been a prodigious one. . . .' "

Peter interrupted, "But I told you he grew the beard after he died."

Stephy said, "You know something? That's almost a perfect description of Peter. Especially the eyes. And that big head of hair. Look at that picture again, doesn't that look like Peter?"

"Don't you think you're being a little far-fetched?" I asked.

"Be quiet, Stephy," Peter growled. "Don't talk foolishness."

"Well," she teased, "don't you think you could be a reincarnation of Beethoven?"

"Don't put things like that in his head," I told her.

"That's right," Peter agreed. "What I have is not reincarnation. I call it inspiration. I go now, play the organ."

"Will you play some Beethoven for us?" I asked.

"No. I don't know Beethoven. I play where my hands go."

"Peter, you do know that the man there in the picture is Beethoven?"

"No. I don't know. I tell you already!" He was shouting again. "But you said he was the one you saw and talked to, and it was his music you heard. . . . That man in the picture *is* Beethoven. You understand?"

"Yes, if you say so. But I don't know his music here, I only hear it up there in that other world. . . ." Then he stalked off moodily into the organ room and began warming up the organ.

I went in cautiously and asked, "Do you mind if we listen?" He shrugged. Sure. "Do you mind if we call Kathryn and let her listen and tell us what you're playing?"

"Okay," he said absently. As he began playing, Stephy attached an apparatus from the tape recorder to the telephone and dialed Kathryn.

Following are Miss Grayson's transcribed words:

"That's Puccini. . . . He plays a lot of tenor arias which Caruso sang. Mostly Puccini and some Bizet. . . . That's Schubert's 'Ave Maria' now. . . . Now it's the Bach-Gounod 'Ave Maria.' . . . Wait—there's the tenor aria from *Tosca*. . . . Not all of it, just bits and pieces . . . Now he's going into Tschaikovsky . . . and now it's something else . . . This is 'Un Bel Dì' from *Madame Butterfly* . . . now it's *Turandot* . . . Puccini. . . .

"Now it's a combination of *Butterfly*, 'Come Back to Sorrento,' and 'O Sole Mio.' He plays a lot of Italian folk songs. . . . There —that one's a Russian song. . . . It's 'O, Chichornia,' but with a Latin beat. That's peculiar. What's that knocking I hear . . . ?"

STEPHY: "Peter just turned on the knob for the drums."

MISS GRAYSON: "It sounds like drumming from outer space. . . . Now he's playing 'Those Were the Days,' another one based on a Russian folk song. . . . There's some from Tchaikovsky's Fifth. . . . But I don't recognize any Beethoven. I've never heard

him play any Beethoven. . . . Why don't you put the picture in
front of him on the organ and see what happens?"

I brought in the Groves book, propped it up on the organ, with
the Beethoven picture in front of him. Again a physical change
came over him as he gently rubbed the face in front of him with
his fingertips and began playing with great passion and sadness.
There was a mystical tone in some of the passages, and a haunting
familiarity in others—like an elusive butterfly-fragment of melody
you've heard somewhere and cannot recapture. At one point,
when he pushed the button for horns, I was vaguely reminded of
those slow, swelling, other-worldly horns at the end of the trio of
Beethoven's great and powerful Eroica. But it wasn't Eroica.
Peter seemed in a state of total mental absorption, almost as
though he had been lifted strangely out of time and into eternity.
Then suddenly his hands and his music became agitated. He
began pounding at chords, pushing and pulling various buttons,
finally slammed a harshly discordant chord, and said, "Something's wrong. My hands go no more."

Into the telephone, Kathryn Grayson asked, "Was that the A
chord he was hitting? [None of us knew.] I think it was the A
chord that Beethoven had trouble with when he was going deaf.
Peter has probably picked up on his deafness. The A would come
in wrong. That's why he couldn't go on. I don't think it was actually Beethoven, at least not from any of his works that I know,
but it certainly had a distinct Beethoven mood and quality," she
added. "Now, what's he doing? There are those drums from outer
space again. . . ."

Peter was back with his happy Latin beat again, and in a hap-
pier mood himself. He began talking as he played.

"When I bought this organ, they told me I get fifteen lessons
free. And I said to them, you can keep the lessons, just put the
thing on [hook it up], and they did, and I am sitting there in the
store and I play. They ask me where I learn to play like that and I
say I have never studied, I just play. But they didn't believe me.

"People have told me that when I hear the song, the melody
that I play, I should put the notes down on paper. I could not do
that, I do not know the notes. I hear it all in my head first, then it

comes out my hands. . . . Come, I play you now my burial song. . . . I only play it on the piano. . . ."
He left the organ and went to the piano in his living room. He began playing a slow, heavy piece with melodic overtones. (A friend of mine later identified part of it, from the tape, as another Italian folk song, "La Spagnola.")
"Where did you get that and why do you call it the burial song?" I asked.
"I don't know where I got it. But I call it the burial song because it has the sadness and also the light. You see, when somebody dies, it is sadness. . . . You play heavier chords . . . like this. . . . But at time of dying, you go to the light . . . you go up, up, up on the chords, like this. . . . This is to show you have heard beautiful music somewhere else. . . ."
"Could you play this same burial song again?" I asked.
"I think so, but maybe you hear a difference. It's not the same every time. . . . It's what I hear, what I feel, what I see. I hear it and my hands are there and it goes."
"And you don't know what the keys or the chords are?"
"No, only what I feel from the body."
"Have you ever been to an opera, Peter?"
"No, I don't like opera and I don't like plays. But I have seen an opera once in a movie. It was *Pagliacci*. . . . Now I'm tired. I don't play any more and I don't want to talk any more."
He arose and left the room. The session was over. I instructed Stephy to round up the art books for our next meeting. And I made a mental note to myself to call Ana Kaneel.

{9}

The Artist—Part I

Certainly art, so far as we can judge it, has not yet discovered in this darkness what it is that holds all men together and could give expression to their psychic wholeness. . . . Great art till now has always derived its fruitfulness from the myth, from the unconscious process of symbolization which continues through the ages and which, as the primordial manifestation of the human spirit, will continue to be the root of all creation in the future. . . .
What can art tell us about our own unconscious feelings?

C. G. JUNG
The Undiscovered Self

I CALLED ANA KANEEL AND SAID, "PETER DOESN'T REMEMBER painting in Holland. How do you know he was a painter?"

"Oh, of course he was painting there. While he was in the hospital. He gave me one of his paintings. And the strange thing is—it's an exact replica of . . . wait a minute, let me think. . . ."

I waited a moment while she thought. Then she spelled it out for me, a Dutch name I had never heard of, but I attached no special significance to this, as there were many Dutch names and Dutch artists who were missing from my repertoire of esoteric knowledge.

"I still have the painting," Miss Kaneel said. "You will see it when you come for my Indonesian dinner. When will you come? Soon, I hope."

"Yes, soon," I said.

I tucked the piece of paper with the Dutch artist's name into my Peter Hurkos tote bag, and moments later I was riding over Laurel Canyon with Stephy to Studio City.

When we arrived, Peter was sitting at the table peeling potatoes, with Gloria Ann in the highchair beside him. He was in a jovial mood.

"You'll stay for dinner tonight. I cook the dinner," he said. "If we wait for Stephy to cook, we will never eat. I'll fix you a nice steak and mashed potatoes."

He bounced up and down, back and forth, between the studio–den table and the kitchen, peeling potatoes, pounding the steaks, chopping vegetables from his garden for the salad.

This was not exactly the time for working, but I tentatively tossed a casual question at him, while deliberately studying some of his paintings on the wall.

"Your colors are all very intense, Peter . . . very strong and vivid and beautiful. Do you happen to remember any famous artists you saw up there—in that other world?"

"Sure. Very famous Dutch painter." He startled us by saying it without hesitation, or going off into his usual meditative mood. "His name was Van Khôkh. . . . Here, I write it for you. . . ."

He stopped pounding his steaks, lumbered over to the table, reached for pencil and paper, and wrote—or printed—almost illegibly but not quite:

VAN GOG

Of course it was Van Gogh, and he had pronounced the name properly in Dutch—Van Khôkh. It was reasonable to assume that no one, certainly not a born Dutchman like Peter, could go through life without knowing about Van Gogh. There was nothing psychically revealing about this, even when Peter said, "Sure, I saw him up there. It had to be. Otherwise where did I get my beautiful colors in my paintings?"

Van Gogh, of course, became famous for his brilliantly colored paintings, works of extraordinary beauty and intensity. It has been said of him, "Perhaps no painter has expressed so poignantly as Van Gogh the rapture of mere vision." And perhaps no one has recaptured more of this feeling on canvas than Peter Hurkos, although whether it came from here or that other world—who knows? It would be natural for him to identify with Van Gogh.

Peter was surprisingly flippant about it. "You know he was a mad man, too, like me," he said, peeling his last potato. When it was all peeled and white, he held the potato in both hands, gave it a long kiss and patted it, then dropped it with loving care into a crockery bowl with the others.

"Why did you kiss the potato?" I asked.

"I always kiss my vegetables and my plants," he said, "and I always talk to them and sing to them. That way they grow healthy and strong for me. You cannot make life without giving life."

His earnestness, his childlike simplicity of mind, his utter belief in what he was saying never ceased to amaze me. It was something to marvel at. And of course it had to be only coincidence that, when I was doing my homework on Van Gogh later, I learned that among his earliest paintings of note was one called "The Potato Eaters."

After dinner we pinned Peter down to the art books.

"We want to know who the painter was you saw up there."

"I don't know," he said. "Sometimes the voices were all mixed up coming at me. Sometimes he was speaking in Dutch, sometimes Italian. But I saw paint brushes through him. I saw him mixing his own paints with beautiful colors. And sometimes I see round things, like domes or ceilings or architecture. This man do many things. But what I saw is the color, the clouds.

"The amazing thing, when they sing, all had one voice, but

different upper and lower. Children had same voices as the father, everybody the same. I try many times to imitate the voices but I cannot. Same with the painting. I tried a long time ago to imitate the colors that I saw there but I cannot."

Peter, you told us you got your musical inspiration from the composer in the other world. Where do you get your inspiration to paint?

"I don't know. From somewhere, but I don't know. I never copy anything. You know that."

You told us that when you play music you hear it and feel it, and then your hands go over the keyboard. Do you hear a voice or do you see a picture when you start to paint?

"I see a picture. You should know that."

You paint with your fingers. Does someone or something take your hand and guide you over the canvas?

"I never know what I'm going to paint. . . . The same with the music. Right . . . ? It leads me . . . but I always start with the clouds."

Do you know why you start with the clouds?

"I try to find the clouds I saw in the other world. The clouds we have here, they are completely different. They are normal clouds. That's why I never start with anything else. . . . I try to find those other clouds."

But why are the skies you paint always so troubled when you are trying to capture that other world which you say was so beautiful?

"It *was* beautiful. . . . But when I am here with my own mind in this world and I mix up the clouds down here with the others. . . . Sometimes I find the most beautiful peace, and sometimes a lot of sadness in the clouds."

We placed one of the art books in front of Peter and began thumbing through the pages. "Tell us if you see anything that looks like what you saw up there."

He stopped at a section of Jacob van Ruisdael's landscapes and said, "See? There are my clouds. This is how I paint. . . . I have power on all my clouds."

Did he recognize the painter's name or had he seen his paintings before?

"No . . . but these are my clouds."

He turned a few pages, stopped again, and said, "This is very strange. . . . Let me show you something. . . . Tess, where is my coloring book?"

Tess brought his sketch pad to him. Peter opened it to a pencil sketch he had done of a landscape dominated by a large oak tree, the figure of a little man resting on its gnarled trunk, and a pastoral stretch of trees and dunes beyond. It was almost an exact replica of the reproduction in the book in front of him, a painting by Jan Van Goyen titled "Landscape with Two Oaks."

I was sure that he had copied it, and he knew this from the tone of my voice.

"When did you do this sketch, Peter?"

"About a year ago."

"How long have you had this book?"

"I never look in books!" he said gloomily.

"No one else will believe you on this, Peter."

"I swear on my daughter, I have never looked in the books, I don't read books, you know that! I showed it to you but I never saw that painting before. You don't believe me? . . . I go now."

He stalked out of the room, as angry as I have ever seen him. Stephy and Tess assured me that he had never opened the art books. It was some time before we could persuade Peter to come out and sit down with us again.

Meanwhile, we had read the brief note in small type beneath the painting:

JAN VAN GOYEN . . . Leyden, 1596–The Hague, 1656. "Landscape with Two Oaks" . . . Oil on canvas; 34¾ × 43½. Initialed and dated: "V G 1641." In the Locoste sale, Dordrecht, 1832; it belonged to the Cabinet J. Rombouts in the same city. Bequest of L. Dupper Wz. of Dordrecht in 1870.

Dordrecht . . . Peter's home town in Holland. I quickly fumbled in my tote bag and found the folded sheet of paper with the Dutch name that Ana Kaneel had spelled out for me. No, it was not Van Goyen.

Peter eventually came back and joined us. He seemed to be in a calmer, more co-operative mood now, but I treaded gently.

"I believe you about your picture, Peter, about not looking in the book—"

He interrupted, "I never lie to you. You know that."

"Yes, I know that. But I want to ask you something. This painting belongs to someone in Dordrecht."

"Dordrecht? How do you know?"

"It says so, right here." I read it to him. "Do you remember maybe ever seeing this painting in Dordrecht? In some art collection or a museum?"

"No. I never saw that painting before."

"Did you have any paintings or reproductions in your home in Dordrecht?"

"No. Nothing. We were very poor. We did not have a piano even."

"Did you ever go to any museums in Dordrecht?"

"No. We don't have museums in Dordrecht. I don't like museums. Once in New York I went to see the mummies. The other time with Stephy in Paris."

"I took him to the Louvre," Stephy said.

"To see the 'Mona Lisa.'" Peter laughed. "I didn't like it."

"Did you see anything like this painting—up there—in the other world?"

"Well, that's where I get all my inspiration, from the other world."

"Can you remember when you first started painting, after your fall?"

"Yes, I have already told you. Not in Holland. Not after I came from unconscious in the hospital. But in Maine with Dr. Puharich. Only small paintings then. First time I ever painted a big picture, it hangs right here. Jesus and Moses. Come, I'll show you. I started to paint the devil and it came out Moses. I did it at the time of my divorce from my wife, when she threw me out of the house and I was very upset. . . ."

He led us into the organ room and stopped in front of a large painting that I had seen in passing many times before and sometimes had vaguely wondered about. It looked like a religious picture to me, a painting of Christ with his crown of thorns, although the plaque with its title said MOSES. Peter is not of an orthodox religious bent. Although there is a distinct spiritual quality that comes through in all of his work—his paintings, his music, his simplistic philosophy—he is not one to spend time on purely religious paintings. In his entire collection, numbering into the hundreds, he has done only three that could be regarded as even ostensibly religious paintings.

"But they were not meant to be religious paintings at all. Just came out that way," he insists. "They are symbolic."

One is called "Father Forgive Them for They Know Not What They Do"—a large, long picture of Christ standing with bowed head. "I painted that one a few years ago when they were bombing the world, destroying the world, and the Lord punished the people," Peter explained.

The other two were painted during the time of his trouble with his second wife who divorced him. One is a painting of Jesus rising from the cross toward a filmy triangle of light, and looking down on a scene of great turbulence, a burning city with houses and churches falling apart.

"See the churches, the false churches falling apart," Peter pointed out. "That's the rotten, stinking world, everything falling apart . . . a mess . . . Jesus was not interested in this world any more . . . so he goes up, up to the light. That is symbolic. It is the way I felt then. I hated this world."

But the most vivid and puzzling reflection of his feelings about the world at that time is in his painting called "Moses," which started out to be the devil.

He recalled with bitterness how it happened.

"I did it at the time of my divorce from my wife, when she threw me out of the house. . . . I was very upset. . . . I was so hateful with everything and then I got very drunk . . . and I felt like I wanted to paint something very bad. . . . I am going to paint the devil, I said. My sketching books were at home but my paints were in the car. And there was a lot of lumber and sticks around the motel because they were building onto it.

"So I got a big piece of wood, like this. . . . Here, I show you."

He removed the "Moses" from the wall, turned it over, and tapped on it. "See, it is wood, not canvas. I have no canvas there. I took this from the lumber pile and I put it on the bed and I started to paint with a small piece of wood, like a stick. . . . Look, here is where I used the stick of wood and here is my finger, right here. . . . That's how I did the eye, with my finger, with a little bit of white on it. . . .

"But I painted mostly with the stick. I painted, I painted, I painted like a wild man, all different colors, and I was full of hate while I painted. I was saying, Why did she do this to me? Why does my wife want to divorce me? Why does she take my child away? WHY? What did I do wrong? I was not in love with anybody else. I am trying to be a good man, a good father. . . . But my wife was frightened about my gift. She did not understand it. How can I take my gift back? How? How?

"Already I have lost my first wife in Holland because of my gift. Then I come to America and I was happy here, but now I was losing my wife and baby again. Why? I hated this world and I wanted to go back to that other world where I was before. . . . So I painted and painted, and I was drunk and I said, You old devil, I will show you are a bad man. . . . And then I fell asleep. . . . It was early morning, and I was so tired, exhausted. . . .

"When I woke up there was paint everywhere in the room . . . all over the bedspread. . . . And the painting was on the floor. I looked at it and when I saw what I had painted, I was frightened, I wanted to run away. . . . I was painting the devil but the way it turned out, it didn't look like the devil."

This began one of the low points in Peter's life. He went through a traumatic few years, and not until he moved to California, met Stephy, and resumed his painting could he bring himself to look at his "devil" again.

He had told Stephy all the circumstances of how he came to paint it. Then one day they brought it out and showed it to an artist friend who said it looked like Moses. So Stephy named it "Moses" and persuaded Peter to hang it with his others.

There can be no doubt that the face of his Moses reflects the inner turbulence of the man who painted it. The colors are splattered, wild, as Peter describes them, as though splashed and jabbed on by a man in a violent attack of madness. The face is upturned in agony, the mouth is open and distorted, and in a certain light his eyes are blinded with tears.

Stephy insists that she actually saw him weeping once. "See, his eyes are all blind here," she points out. "That's where the tears came out. I had them analyzed. They were a saline solution, just like real tears," she said.

There have been sporadic reports of "weeping" pictures and statues which are dear to the hearts of the mystics. I personally have never seen one. I told Stephy to let me know the next time she saw Moses weeping. . . .

I did, however, experience a strangely uncomfortable feeling as I looked at the "Moses" from a distance, at a certain angle. His face bore a faint resemblance to the shadowy, upturned profile of the bearded man in "Mur Woods." Or was it only my imagination?

I asked Peter to bring the little painting out of the bedroom so we could study it again in the light.

Meanwhile, I casually thumbed through the index of the art books on the table, searching for the name of the Dutch painter that Ana Kaneel had spelled out for me. It was not there, in any of the books. . . .

Tess was telling me how Peter paints. She had worked with him for twelve years and had watched him paint hundreds of times, usually to relax after working on a case.

"Wherever we happened to be, I would always have to go out and buy him canvases and paints," she said. "That was the only way he could relax and go to sleep, especially after working on a police case. But many times he was too disturbed over the case, and his mind was all confused, and this would come out in his paintings. There was always a kind of turbulence in them.

"He always paints those troubled skies. . . . Let me tell you something that happened. One night in Syracuse, Peter did a painting before he went down to work, and when he came back to his room the painting had completely changed. All the colors had run together, just like someone came into the room and ran their hands over it or something, and mixed it all up. When Peter saw it, he was wild. He told me to get it out of there, fast, so I took it to my room. But he wouldn't let me keep it. He didn't want it in his sight. He didn't even want it in the hotel, so I had to get rid of it, throw it away."

"Could the colors have run together because of the way it was standing?"

"No, it was in oils and it couldn't have run," Tess said. "Sometimes he paints on a table, sometimes on the floor," she added. "He can paint anywhere. He likes to paint on the floor. He paints sideways, upside down, however he feels like it."

Peter had re-entered the room and heard her. "I told you how I paint," he said. "Why do you think I have so many canvases? If I get an inspiration in the middle of the night, I get out of bed and I do it. . . . The force wants me to do it, my hands have to do it. . . . I am not a painter, I am not an artist. . . . My hands can't help where they go. . . . Here, you take it . . . the man with the beard. . . ." He gave me the "Mur Woods" painting with the face in the clouds. "I have to rest now," he said. "Don't want to think. You get me all screwed up with the paintings. I go too deep into them."

{10}

The Artist—Part II

What can art tell us about our unconscious feelings?

C. J. JUNG

WE STUDIED THE LITTLE "MUR WOODS" PAINTING AGAIN FROM many angles of light. The bearded figure was still there, his arm around the little boy's shoulders, and the boy's face was still there, framed with the black curly hair and the flowing white scarf around his neck.

We could see them only in certain lights but they had not gone away. They were there and they were still the same. And we could see them as distinctly now as before. We were not merely hallucinating.

The figure of the man was not as sharply outlined but the predominant features had not changed—the upturned face, open mouth, and anguished eyes. His face had a softer, more ethereal quality than the face of the tortured Moses, but there was a similarity. The resemblance, however, could scarcely be interpreted as having any special psychic significance, beyond the fact that both paintings reflected a style, a mood, and the subconscious feelings of a man who genuinely believed that he had seen the face in another world.

Far more puzzling was the child's face, remarkably tranquil by contrast, reposed, peaceful, and half-smiling, and looking out from the clouds with half-closed quizzical eyes, as if asking, "Why are you staring at me?"

We took the little "Mur Woods" and went roaming from room to room, comparing the clouds to those in Peter's other paintings.

"You see, this is what I mean by his troubled skies," said Tess, indicating several of them. "He usually paints this kind of sky after he has worked on a case. When he's peaceful, when he just feels like painting, then he does this kind. . . . But look at them, all of them . . . you can't find any faces in any of these clouds. This is the only one."

"When he first painted it," Stephy added, "I thought it was very pretty. And I liked it because we had been there. There's a place called Mur [Muir] Woods up near San Francisco, you know. . . . It's beautiful. . . . I didn't know about the little boy's face being there until Peter woke me up one night about three weeks later and showed it to me. And we didn't even see the man with the beard then. A friend pointed that one out to us. . . ."

"Were you with him while he was painting it?" I asked Stephy.

"Oh, sure. I saw him do it. It didn't take him very long."

"What kind of mood was he in while he was painting?"

"He was in a very happy mood. We both were. I had just found out that I was pregnant and he had always wanted to start another family. He was on cloud nine!" said Stephy.

"That's the truth, I was on cloud nine," announced Peter, coming into the room to join us. "Stephy's a good little mother, even if she never learn to cook." He gave her a pat on the head, then sat down in his favorite spot—facing the TV set—across the table from me.

He looked at me sharply and said, "You want to know something—why I need Stephy? Because she is never afraid of my gift, like the others. It's the God's truth. She's not afraid. Ask Stephy."

"Well, I might be, just a little sometimes," said Stephy, "but I'd never let Peter know it."

The strange May-December marriage of Peter and Stephy has intrigued many of their friends. He is thirty-three years older than Stephy, but still virile, handsome, physically attractive. Stephy came into his life at a time when he needed someone to give him something to live for—if he had to continue living in this world.

It was Stephy who helped him find himself again after his broken marriage, and taught him to live with the gift he could not understand.

I had known Peter long before Stephy knew him—from those early days when he was being exploited in this country in the name of "research in parapsychology," when he had a simple, childlike belief that certain persons were interested in his gift and would either help him get rid of it or tell him how to handle it.

"I was willing to work six months in America to find out about my gift and I was very happy maybe to find why. I didn't care about coming to America. I only wanted to find out what was wrong with my head."

I had known the wife and the baby daughter and the circumstances that had caused Peter to paint his "devil."

After that he drifted out to the West Coast, a nonentity, a complete derelict in spirit, dejected, rejected, and about ready to take his own life and go back to that other world when he met Stephy.

She was a mere child then. But he had just lost one daughter, by divorce, so he acquired another.

What started as a father-daughter relationship soon emerged from that chrysalis as a courtship that led to marriage. Stephany has not only accepted his gift but helped him put it to practical use in ways not always acceptable to the academic community of parapsychologists. But it pays the bills. And as Stephy says, "Why shouldn't Peter be paid for his work—like any other specialist? Do you know any better psychic specialist than Peter?"

Stephy perhaps has done more to restore and preserve Peter's sanity in his hallucinatory world than anyone else. She believes in him implicitly.

We guardedly brought Peter back to the art books in front of him but he seemed uninterested. He flicked through pages of paintings and photographs half-heartedly, and did not identify with any of them as he had with the composers.

Peter, you said you saw a painter up there, a man with paint brushes and buckets of paint. Did he talk to you? What did he say?

"He said the same thing, what they all said, that I was going to have a gift. But he said my gift would develop in different ways."

He didn't tell you what those ways were?

"Not specific, no. But this man did many things—painter, sculptor, architect, engineer, everything. He is more than a painter. Very intellectual. Mathematician, scientist, he is a genius from this world. I see everything through him . . . painting, churches, scenery, nature study, submarines, guns and cannon. . . . He is not just a painter like Van Khôkh . . . a more powerful man in this world. Up there he was like all the other jurymen with beards. . . ."

We opened a book to a picture of the "Mona Lisa."

What do you feel about this?

"I saw that in the museum with Stephy." He shrugged. " 'Mona Lisa.' Right, Stephy? I don't like it. That is nothing in my style. . . . I don't paint figures . . . I don't paint nudes. . . . I paint scenery most, and water, trees, and clouds. Everything I paint is power. . . ."

Do you know who painted the "Mona Lisa"?

"No. An Italian painter, I think. I don't want to look now at any more pictures." He pushed the book aside.

We closed all the books, and Tess, intuitively knowing Peter's moods, carted them off to the study and out of his sight.

But I couldn't refrain from asking, "Peter, do you know who Leonardo da Vinci was?"

"Oh, sure. He was a painter and sculptor. Or was he just a painter? Maybe it was that guy Angelo [Michelangelo]. . . ." He wasn't interested in art at the moment. He walked over and turned on the television.

Stephy said, "Tony Bennett thinks there's more da Vinci in Peter's work than anyone else. Not the style, but the power and feeling." (Tony Bennett is the singer, an art connoisseur and collector, and a friend of theirs.)

Da Vinci's best-known paintings, of course, are his "Mona Lisa" and "Last Supper," and nothing in any of Peter's work bears the remotest resemblance to either of them.

Still, there were certain characteristics about the artist on that celestial jury Peter remembered from his out-of-body trip that might make you wonder.

Consider, for instance, the following brief notes on da Vinci compared with Peter's description of his artist up there.

LEONARDO DA VINCI (1452–1519). Italian painter, sculptor, architect, engineer, scientist, poet, and musician. A universal genius and one of the greatest intellects in the history of mankind. Worked as an engineer as well as a designer of costumes and scenery for court entertainment in Milan. . . . Made sketches of churches, painted the murals and ceiling pictures of the Sforza castle in Milan. . . . Served as military engineer to Caesar Borgia. . . . He left no architectural works but his sketches for buildings and even whole cities were influential for his contemporaries. . . . Experimented with various mechanical devices, including guns and cannon, flying machines, parachutes, hydraulic works, submarines, and spiral staircases. [At least Peter hadn't mentioned spiral staircases yet!] . . . In his notebooks there are some 5,000 pages of sketches and comments that reveal his concern with anatomy, botany and mathematics, plant studies and landscapes. His favorite motif: fidelity to nature.

It is indeed awesome to speculate what might happen to a man who goes plummeting toward an untimely death, only to find himself confronted in his out-of-body world by no less than a bona-fide da Vinci.

If I were writing science fiction I could happily assume that it was da Vinci who created all those other-world igloos, domed roofs, ethereally floating half shells and flying circles that Peter got caught up in. For it was da Vinci who painted the murals on the domed ceilings of churches, and left a legacy of architectural dreams of domed cities.

If we let our imagination take wings (as da Vinci did with his flying machines), he would be the master architect of that celestial city.

Who else would have designed that domed marble meeting hall for the anointed nine men on the celestial jury?

But this was only a flight of fancy, not out-of-body.

Peter at the moment was very much alive and preoccupied with TV.

When the opportune time came, I asked him, "Did anyone— up there—ever tell you specifically what your gift would be [I was still uncomfortable with that word gift] . . . that you would be a psychic, and that you would be working on police cases down here as a psychic?"

"Yes. Definite. Two," he said. Anticipating my question, he added, "Don't ask me who. I tell you I don't know who the men were when they came. They never tell me their names. I never tell you what I don't know for sure. I only tell you what I do know, and what I hear and what I saw.

"But I tell you one man I saw up there was a very bad man, dirty like a pig under the white, and I said, I don't want your gift, you dirty pig. You go back to that dirty hell, don't send me back!

"We don't talk about it now. Later. He makes me too upset."

{11}

The Healer

PETER'S BEARDED GUIDES IN THE OTHER WORLD NEVER LET HIM ROAM far out of their sight. As he told it, or as I reconstructed it from his fragmentary recall, the guides would appear, reappear, and disappear, in shadowy, formless luminosity—like ectoplasm at a seance.

Until now he had never seen any of them close up again after his first meeting in the domed marble hall. But he was always aware of their presence.

One day he was sitting alone in the mountains near a fresh-water spring when he was approached by a bearded man whose face he did not recognize from the jury table. It was different from the others and not as clean or as kind.

"He was a very bold man," said Peter. "He came right up to me and pointed his finger against me and he said, 'I know who you are and you don't belong here and you are going to be punished.'

"He was a big man. He was dressed in white, transparent like the others, but I could see through and he was dirty. His beard was very, very messy. I did not like him. I said, 'I don't know who you are. Who are you? How do you know I am going to be punished?'

"He said, 'No *poni mai*.' And I said, 'What language is that?' He didn't answer. Then he sat down beside me. . . ."

Peter stopped, hesitated. He looked as though he was about to go off into a semitrance state of recall that was not going to be pleasant.

"Before you go on, Peter, what were those words the man said in the language you didn't understand?"

"*No poni mai, no poni mai,*" he repeated. He printed the words on a piece of paper for us.

"Do you know what language it is, or what it means?"

"No. I ask but he didn't answer me. Could be it means, 'You be punished.' I don't know."

"What language did he speak the rest of the time?"

"I don't know. Russian maybe. He told me he was from Russia. But I think mostly he spoke by telepathy."

"He said he was from Russia?"

"Yes. He said he was from a little farm close by a small village in Russia. And he told me he knew I loved farming, too. I said, 'How do you know that?' And he said, 'I know all about you in that world you are from, and you are going back and you will be hurt in that world, you will have many people against you, who don't believe in you, but you have a job to do.' I told him the only job I know was painting houses. He said, 'But when you go back you will have a different work to do, what the people here and the Big Master tell you to do.'

"I ask him, 'Who is the Big Master?' And he say, 'Nobody knows. But it's the Big Master who makes the decision.' I ask him would I get to meet the Big Master, but he did not answer me.

I'm pretty sure it was not God or Jesus," Peter said. "He would be on another planet."

"What else did he tell you about himself?" I asked. "Or about Russia?"

"Well, I have to tell you," said Peter, in a tone of disgust, "he said he was a very powerful man in the world I come from because he had a great gift, he was a healer. I thought how could he be a healer if he didn't wash himself, dirty pig. He tell me he heal lots of people, big important people, and he was powerful and famous.

"He said, 'I tried to do good in that world you came from but I was hurt because the people didn't understand me, same as you will be. The people, the world, everybody tried to destroy me. I did many good things for the world and they tried to kill me . . . but they couldn't kill me. . . . They tried many times and finally they did.'

Peter continued, "He told me that God had given him his gift of healing and that it was very powerful, he could cure many diseases, especially blood diseases, and nobody could kill him until that job was finished. He said they tried many times to kill him and couldn't.

"So I asked him then, how did he die? He said, 'I didn't die, my air was cut off, and my lungs were full of water, but I was not murdered by poison and I was not murdered by guns, I was murdered by water. It was the water that stopped me from breathing. I was attacked nine times but no one was able to kill me.' . . . That's what he told me," Peter said.

By now Peter could have been getting his information by telepathy from my own mind instead of from the bearded man up there. On second thought, no, I only remembered all those details as Peter mentioned them but my mind could have confirmed them for him. And certainly now there was no doubt in my mind who the man was, and if Peter didn't already know his identity, then he easily could have plucked it from me by telepathy.

I asked him to explain how the man was "murdered by water."

"He said they put him in a bag . . . and he was frozen in . . .

half under snow and ice. . . . It was cold. . . . It was snowing. . . . He tried to get out but he couldn't. He was in a sack and couldn't breathe. He was frozen in under the ice, and he said he was in the darkness then. I told him I was in the darkness, too, and he said, 'Your darkness was different from my darkness. My darkness was in a bag and I could not get out. You got out of your darkness, nobody killed you, nobody after you, you were not killed and that's why they're going to send you back.' "

"Wait a minute, Peter," I said. "How do you know that about the ice and snow, and his being frozen under the ice?"

"How do you think I know? That's what he told me, that it was cold and snowing and he was running after they shoot him and poison him, and he still thought nobody could hurt him, but they did because they put him in the bag under the ice."

He paused, then added in a tone of pouty belligerence, "You don't believe me, how I know it, I tell you something else how I know. I saw the icicle on his beard."

This was too much. Tess and Stephy and I cast quick furtive glances at one another in our own telepathic communication: *Don't laugh!*

We knew he was dead serious, and he could be easily offended, and explosive. He had been (for him) reasonably patient with us so far. So, let him have an icicle on the man's beard.

But I decided it was time to call a halt and do some checking. I felt certain that Peter was picking up by telepathy—or preknowledge?—the vibrations of Russia's notorious healer Rasputin. But I had only a scant recollection of the details of his death. I didn't even know the month in which he died, whether it was during the winter or summer.

While Peter went in and played the organ, I consulted with Stephy and went over their meager library of books (most of them came with the house when they bought it), none of which contained any references to Rasputin.

I then telephoned my ever-vigilant Vera (my assistant) and asked her to look up Rasputin in The Columbia Encyclopedia and read it to me. I later copied it, and for others who don't remember, here it is:

RASPUTIN, GRIGORI YEFIMOVICH. Rus. 1872–1916, Russian monk,* a notorious figure at the court of Nicholas II. He was an illiterate peasant and a debauchee, affiliated with a mystic sect akin to revivalism. Because of his magnetism and because of his apparent miraculous cure of the young tsarevich, who suffered from hemophilia, Rasputin gained complete hold over Empress Alexandra Feodorovna and, through her, over the emperor. The statesmen and ministers who tried to oppose him were removed from their posts; those who remained were his tools. The court was plunged into a nearly insane atmosphere of mysticism and the imperial family obeyed the slightest whims of the "Holy man" while Russia suffered crushing defeats in the First World War. It was suspected that the empress, who was German by birth, and Rasputin made their own use of the secret information which Nicholas was too weak to withhold from them. The liberal section of the Duma also feared that Rasputin was working with the ultrareactionary clique for a separate peace with Germany. In Dec., 1916, a group of conspirators, all belonging to the highest nobility, killed Rasputin at the palace of Prince Yussupov. Rasputin's constitution was tough: a generous dose of poison failed to produce any visible effect, and the terrified conspirators riddled him with bullets and drowned him in the frozen Neva for good measure. During the February Revolution of 1917, Rasputin's corpse was exhumed and burned by the mob.

In October 1965, in New York, Prince Felix Yussupov, then seventy-nine, described how he first gave Rasputin poisoned cakes, tea, and wine, which had failed to kill him, and then shot him twice, after which the "Mad Monk" leaped up and tried to choke him. Rasputin then ran out into the courtyard with his assassins after him. When their bullets still failed to kill him, Prince Felix finally beat him to death, he said, with what he described as a night stick, and then dumped his body in the Neva River. The Russian prince maintained that his only motive for killing Raspu-

* Isaac Don Levine, leading Russian authority and longtime personal friend of mine, says The Columbia Encyclopedia is wrong in describing Rasputin as a monk, without quotation marks. A bona-fide monk is an ordained member of a religious order, like a nun. In Russia, Rasputin was called a *staretz*, which means a holy pilgrim. See Levine's description on following pages.

tin, the reputed power behind the last Russian czar, was repugnance over the monk's debauchery and not for any political reasons. (The New York *Times*, October 16–21, 1965.)

Prince Yussupov's candid account of his leading role in plotting the assassination and in carrying it out became a best-selling book in the 1930s and has been the subject of movies and TV dramas.

A little-known but intriguing account of one of history's most notorious lechers and his role as the real ruler in the court of Czar Nicholas II is told by America's foremost Sovietologist, Isaac Don Levine, in his book *The Russian Revolution*, published in 1917, and now probably available only through rare book dealers. Levine was then foreign news editor of the old New York *Tribune*. Following are brief excerpts:

GREGORY NOVIKH was born in the village of Pokrovsky in Siberia. . . . The son of a common muzhik, Gregory was absolutely uneducated and illiterate. It was only late in his life, when he became a power in the Court, that he learned to scrawl most ungrammatically and unintelligibly. . . . He early showed himself to be a degenerate even in his native village. He acquired the reputation of a drunkard and a rogue. His disorderly behaviour made him the outcast of the community. . . . His fellow-peasants nicknamed him Grishka, a contemptuous form of Gregory. . . . He became known by the name of Rasputin. . . . Rasputin means a rake, a libertine, a morally irresponsible person. . . . He evidently liked the name so much that he adopted it instead of his original name . . . and proceeded to build his amazing, almost stupefying career of an omnipotent power behind the throne. . . . [He] became a professional "pilgrim" . . . under a religious cloak. His power over women seemed almost superhuman . . . [but] his reputation as a "saint" grew steadily. . . .

Women of noble birth, wives and daughters of the great, visited Rasputin in his village. He taught them that part of his body was divine, and that to be purged of sin it was necessary to unite with him spiritually and physically. It was astounding how popular Rasputin became in high feminine society. His despicable manners did not seem to offend the titled aristocrats who invited him to their homes.

Influential officials later sought his company at the expense of his abominable liberties with their wives or daughters. Like an animal, he ate with his fingers and his disciples would often lick them clean at his command. The men among his followers were mostly seekers for high offices, who would sacrifice almost anything to ingratiate themselves with the muzhik who was becoming a powerful influence behind the throne.

The fascination of the man lay altogether in his eyes. . . . Otherwise he looked simply a common muzhik, with no beauty to distinguish him; a sturdy rogue, overgrown with a forest of dirty, unkempt hair, dirty in person (dirt is holiness in some countries), and disgusting in habits. . . .

To the Court Rasputin was introduced in 1905 as the creator of a new religious cult. The "monk" soon acquired tremendous influence over the Czar and Czarina . . . by his pretensions to wield a miraculous power over the well-being of the Grand Duke Alexis [their son] who was suffering from an incurable illness [hemophilia]. . . . The Czarina had implicit faith in the holiness of the imposter. Rasputin became a member of the Czar's household. . . .

Levine gives a detailed description of Rasputin's political activities, which were closely knit with the fortunes of Russia during the fifteen months preceding the revolution and the overthrow of czarism. Then of Rasputin's death he wrote:

In the early hours . . . a policeman on duty heard the sounds of shots and cries coming from a house belonging to the young Prince Felix Yusupov. . . .

A short while later two motor-cars drove up to the door and into the garden. In one of the cars a large bundle was placed. Beside this bundle a man took his seat and ordered the chauffeur to drive to an island at the mouth of the Neva. Traces of blood were left in the garden. There were also marks of blood on the ice of the frozen Neva where the car had stopped. Near these marks was a freshly made hole. And close to the hole lay a pair of blood-stained rubber shoes.

The bundle that was taken out of the house of Prince Yusupov was the body of Rasputin, the omnipotent monk who had ruled Russia from behind the throne of the Czar. He had been lured by the aristocratic company to the dwelling of the young Prince Yusupov, shot there, carried to the river, and dropped into the hole. The dark forces had received a powerful blow. Their leader was gone. . . .

. . . The body was recovered from the river . . . taken to the pal-

ace where the camarilla [a Mafia type of junta] paid their last re-
spects to the imposter. . . . One of the chief mourners was the Emperor [Nicholas II] . . . who with others carried the silver coffin in
which Rasputin's body had been placed to the burying-ground. The
Czarina and the Court intriguers followed in deep mourning. . . .

"Well, I guess you could have seen an icicle on the man's
beard," I said to Peter when we resumed our session. "Now, have
you ever heard of Rasputin?"

"Sure. You mean Ruspoo'tyin," he said with the Russian pro-
nunciation. It sounds like Roos-pooh-teen, with the accent on the
last syllable, and that is the way Peter pronounced it from there
on. But I would like to make it clear here—again—that Peter
doesn't read books, magazines, or newspapers (I have never seen a
magazine or newspaper in his house), he barely reads enough
English to get his driver's license with Stephy's help (and she
does the driving), although he is not an illiterate, as Rasputin
was.

"He told me, 'I had no education like you had,' that's what he
told me. . . ."

I did not mention to Peter what I had learned about Rasputin
beyond the fact that he was drowned in the frozen river.

"You had read about Rasputin, or heard about him when you
were a small boy in school?" I asked.

"Are you kidding? I never heard about him in school. I was too
young then."

True. Peter would not have been even six years old yet when
Rasputin died. And Peter's schooling from there on was sketchy.

Had he seen him portrayed in the movies or on television?

Again, "Are you kidding? We did not have television then in
Holland. And no, he was never in the movies that I saw. We were
too poor to go to the movies. Except *The Great Caruso*."

"But have you seen him in the movies here, in this country, or
on television?"

"No. But what do you mean? I saw him only when I had my fall. That was 1941," he reminded me.

"Okay, okay. When you saw him then, did you know he was Rasputin?"

"My God, you never listen." He was exasperated again. "How many times do I have to tell you, nobody up there ever said who they were. You say Ruspoo'tyin. How do I know?"

"Do you know the names of any famous Russian men?"

"I know only about the czars, not their names. But they were czars. They were not farmers and they were not healers. He told me he healed the son of the czar, too. He had a blood disease. Then he told me I would make a good healer, too, because my hands and fingers were big and strong like his. He showed me his hands, and I was disgusted, they were so dirty. I told him, I don't want to be a healer and I'm not interested in what you're telling me.

"But he would not stop. He said that when I learned to do healing I must never use rings or metals on my hands, no jewelry at all. It's the power and the energy in the hands, he told me. That's the way he did it. He would look the people in the eye and then touch them and then cross his hands in front of them—like this. [Peter demonstrated] . . .

"He said sometimes he used a shiny object, like a cross, in front of them to make them concentrate or sleep, maybe like in hypnosis or something and then he would heal them. But I think this is all baloney and so we get into big argument."

At this point, Tess interjected a comment: "But, Peter, you always take off your rings and your watch when you're doing a diagnosis, or healing a pain or something. . . ."

"Yes, but I don't get it from this man," he snapped. "I do it because the best thing is without any metals. I know! But this healer said he didn't do it with his eyes only, he had to touch the people, too. And that's why I get mad, and I say, 'How can you touch the people with dirty hands? How can you have your healing power? They could get infection from you.' He said dirty has nothing to do with it, it's the power. He said he looked at people and made the diagnosis and then he touch the people where the illness was, where the pain was, and that was how he healed them. He told me this.

"He said he did not want to wash or shave or take baths . . . no time for taking baths and shaving . . . that was his energy and his power. He said, 'If I wash or shave I lose my power.'

"And then he said to me, 'I'm not sure, but I think they are going to send you back with a different gift, the same as I have, but I have no right to make the decision. That is for the Big Master.

" 'But the reason I came to talk to you is maybe you can be a good healer and wash yourself, too.' And I said, 'Oh, no! I will not be a healer.' And that's when I argued with him and said, 'Why don't you go back where you belong? You don't belong here with everybody clean. Why don't you go wash yourself, you dirty pig . . . you're like an animal.' That's what I told him . . . like an animal he was so dirty.

"I think I made him feel bad. So he told me he was born in a barn in a little village of about three hundred people, and there was not even a road and if he wanted to go walking, he went on his knees in the mud. . . . He said he traveled from village to village, and never took his clothing off, never took a bath, and at first the people were frightened about him but when he got his healing power, everybody came to see him. . . .

"Then he stood up and he said, 'Well it is not my decision but if they send you back with a gift, you are going to be a very lonely man, you are going to fight alone with your gift. *No poni mai.*'†
And then he went away. I think he went to another planet, I don't know."

Peter seemed relieved to have him gone.

"Do you remember the first time you ever heard about Rasputin?" I asked.

"Yes. In Paris." He stopped abruptly as though he didn't want to talk about it.

---

† Isaac Don Levine says this is a Russian phrase. Correct spelling: *ne ponimayu,* meaning "I don't understand." Peter doesn't speak Russian.

"Do you remember what year it was?"

"Yes. It was 1950. *After* my fall," he repeated with emphasis.

"Do you remember who told you about Rasputin?"

"Yes. Madame Simonoff."

"Who was she?"

"She was royalty from the palace of the czar. She told me she danced with Ruspoo'tyin."

"What were you doing in Paris?"

"I was giving a lecture [demonstration] for a benefit for the Red Cross. All the big stars were there . . . like Charles Trenet and Mistinguette. But she wouldn't even talk to me. Why should she? They had never even heard of me, but I gave a good demonstration and I had headlines in the paper."

"Is that when you met Madame What's-her-name?"

"Simonoff. [He spelled it out] She was there and she came backstage to see me. And the first thing she said to me, I never forget it . . . she said, 'If you had a beard, you would look just like Ruspoo'tyin. And you have a great gift . . . like his but different. . . . *Vous êtes formidable, qu'est-ce qu'il a dit.* . . . *Monsieur Ruspoo'tyin . . . c'est la même chose. . . .*'"

"What does that mean?" asked Stephy.

"It means I am big, strong, powerful, that's what she said, like Ruspoo'tyin . . . the same thing. . . . She was interested in me. . . . She ask me to come to her castle and meet her husband. . . . I think he was a general from the Army but I don't think she had relations with her husband. . . . She had relations with Ruspoo'tyin. . . . She told me she danced with him many times when she lived in Moscow, and he was big and strong and powerful and a very nice man but that the women make him crazy, they were always running after him. . . .

"She told me he was a healer and that he had great power and could see through people, like me. . . . And all the time, she was telling me how I reminded her of Ruspoo'tyin, how I am big and strong like him and have the power also. She was always afraid to shake his hand because he was so strong and powerful and she was afraid to shake my hand, too. . . . I think she wanted to go to bed with me. . . ."

He laughed, and Stephy laughed, too. "Well, can you blame her?"

Peter added, as an afterthought, "She was not a bad-looking woman, either, but too pale, white, white face, Russian type. Also I had my wife with me." For a moment he had a rapscallion glint in his eye.

He resumed on a more serious note. "But Madame Simonoff told me one thing she didn't like about Ruspoo'tyin was he was always dirty . . . never changed his clothes . . . always the same coat . . . dark, dirty clothing. . . . She told me also that the prince who killed Ruspoo'tyin lived in Paris only four blocks away. She wanted him to meet me but he didn't want to meet me, he was too frightened. He was so frightened all these years, the prince who killed Ruspoo'tyin, that he locked himself up many years and wouldn't go out, and when he read in the papers that I had a gift, he didn't want to meet me. He was afraid that I was going to kill him. So I never got to meet the prince."

"Did Rasputin tell you about the prince?"

"No. Madame Simonoff told me. The man I saw only told me about the poison and the bullets and the drowning in the bag in the ice."

"Did Madame Simonoff tell you about that, too?"

"No. She only told me what a great man he is and how I remind her of him. She told me I walk like Ruspoo'tyin, only he was heavier, and a strong man."

"Did you tell her you had seen Rasputin—up there—in that other world?"

"No, no, NO! How could I tell her? I didn't know who he was. And I never talk with her about my fall. I never talk with anybody about my fall, only here."

Stephy looked at him thoughtfully and said, "Peter, you know something? I think you should get Rasputin out of your head. He was a very evil man and you don't look like him at all. You're much more like Beethoven and he was a nicer man even if he was temperamental."

"Ya. Ruspoo'tyin no good. That's why he was not on the jury," said Peter.

But Peter had said there was a "healer" on the jury. And there were two who had told him specifically that he would have the gift of a psychic.

{12}

The Seer

THIS IS THE WAY PETER DESCRIBED IT. HE WAS FLYING AROUND ON one of those little (da Vinci) half shells when he encountered the ectoplasmic image (my words, not his) of perhaps the world's greatest seer of all time.

"What kind of man are you?" asked Peter.

"In your world I predicted many things that have come true. I will stay beside you. I will be with you," the man said. "We will have to send you back but you will have a gift, like mine. You will be able to see into the future . . . and the past. . . ."

"I was a house painter and I don't want to go back," Peter told the man. "I don't want to see into the future and the past. I don't want any gift. I want to stay here."

"But your time is not ready for here," he told Peter. "We cannot accept you here yet. You have a long way to go before you are ready for here."

It was only a brief encounter but Peter remembers it vividly. "This man had a mustache and a beard, and he spoke in French and Latin and telepathy. He was very well educated, high intellectual . . . and clean . . . not like the other. He said, 'I will give you the insight and the vision, same like mine, so you can see through things, but you have to believe very strong. . . . No one else will believe you.' . . . I was very upset. . . .

"He said I would do predictions and I said, 'I don't want to do predictions, that is the work of the devil.' He told me if I use it right, it would be for good, to better humanity, but I didn't care about that. All I wanted was to be left alone in that other world. . . . But he was a very fine gentleman. He said when he was living here on this planet where I come from that he was very well known but up there nobody is well known, everybody is the same. . . .

"And then he told me something that really upset me. He said he saw me working with the police, with many crimes when I came back, and I was going to come back as a different person, like a psychic . . . and I said, 'Oh, no, no, in the first place I don't like police and in the second place I'm frightened about them. . . .'"

I interrupted to ask, "Did the man actually use the word 'psychic'?"

"Oh no, no, no. Are you kidding? Nobody in the other world ever used the word 'psychic.' I never even heard that word until I came to this country, and then people had to explain it to me and I know that is what they mean in the other world. That was my gift. Psychic."

The word psychic is derived from the Greek word *psychikos*, meaning "of the soul or life, spiritual." It also means "sensitive to nonphysical forces." Thus, the interchangeability of the terms "psychic" and "sensitive." Peter has been called both.

Did the man who made predictions tell you any of the specific cases you might be working on with the police?

"No. He say nothing specific about that. Only that people would be against me, like the people were against him, so I must believe very strong in my gift, same as he did. He said he was proved right many times and same with me, I would be proved right also. But I said, No, thank you, I did not want any gift."

I opened a book and showed Peter a picture to psychometrize.

Tell me, is this the man you saw?

He ran his fingertips over the picture, then placed a sheet of paper underneath the eyes, moved the paper up and down and said, "Yes. Definite. That is the man I talked to in the half shell. And he was on my jury, too. He was a good man but people didn't appreciate him what he did in this life."

The picture was a photo reproduction of the only known authentic portrait of Nostradamus painted from life by his son, Caesar. (From *The Complete Prophecies of Nostradamus*, translated, edited, and interpreted by Henry C. Roberts.) He had a handsome growth of facial hair—thick sideburns, well-trimmed mustache, and luxuriantly pointed beard. He bore the look of a distinguished "gentleman," as Peter called him—scholarly, aristocratic, and elegant, but again, as with Beethoven, it was the eyes of the man, rather than the beard, that caught Peter's attention.

"You see," he said, "it's this eye [left] that is his normal one. This one [right] is the one that sees into the future. You don't know what it's seeing."

He was right—at least as far as the difference in the eyes was concerned. One seemed to be bright and alert. The other was mesmerically staring into some far-beyond. Like Peter's at times.

Do you know who this man is, Peter?

"No."

It's Nostradamus. Did you ever hear of Nostradamus?

"Sure. He's the man who made big predictions."

Peter's naïve, childlike truthfulness was sometimes even more baffling than his psychic talents.

"But I don't make predictions," he reminded me again.

Do you know anything else about Nostradamus?
"No."
He didn't tell you anything else when you saw him up there?
"No."
Would you be interested—would you like to know something about him?
"No."
Well, I'm going to read to you something about him anyway.
He shrugged and lit another cigar. I read to him bits and pieces from biographical notes that I thought might interest him.

MICHAEL DE NOSTRADAMUS . . . Born 1503, St. Remy, France. [Where Van Gogh was committed to the asylum] . . . Died 1566 . . . Received his early education in medicine and astrology. . . . Studied at Montpellier, the best medical school in France, where they taught a mixture of medicine, alchemy, and magic . . . Had great success in treating plague patients. [But couldn't save his own wife and two children] . . . Traveled widely in France and Italy for about eight years, becoming wealthy from grateful families he had cured of the plague. It was during this period that the gift of prophecy began to manifest itself. . . .

. . . Practiced magic and used rituals which drugged the conscious mind. . . . It is quite well established that he thought in Latin and wrote in French. . . . Might have entered a trancelike state and by automatic writing . . . wrote Latin phrases. . . . Some say he obtained "messages" by semisuspension of consciousness . . . discovered the power of symbols. . . .

He was very obscure . . . Made his predictions in quatrains deliberately so people wouldn't understand them.

Peter interrupted, "What do you mean—quatrain?"
I tried to explain. "It's like four lines of poetry . . . only it's not poetry." And I read:

> About midnight the leader of the army
> Shall save himself, vanishing suddenly,
> Seven years after his fame shall not be blamed,
> And at his return he shall never say yes.

I explained, "This is supposed to mean that Hitler would return alive seven years after his supposed death in 1945."

"Baloney," said Peter.

"But he predicted some very important events. . . . He prophesied that the end of the world will come in the year 7000 . . . when the sun will destroy the earth and again resume its undisputed sway. . . . That means the world is going to be destroyed in the year 7000. . . . Do you believe that, Peter?"

"No. Definite not. The man is cuckoo."

"But you said he was very intelligent. . . . And it says here he was educated in medicine and astrology."

"All the same, cuckoo."

"But you said he was a good man and that he was on your jury —up there."

Peter tapped the picture of Nostradamus again and said, "Yes, yes. Definite. He was one of the jurymen. From the half shell. Very fine gentleman in this world but people didn't appreciate him," he repeated.

As was often the case, Peter didn't seem to connect the name of the man and the biographical notes I read with the man he was talking about in the other world. He had heard of Nostradamus, he knew he made "big predictions," but Peter wasn't interested in predictions. For him none of this bore any relationship to the man whose photo he had psychometrized and identified as the man he met on the half shell.

I never tried to put words in Peter's mouth. I wouldn't have had much luck anyway. It would have been easy for him to pick up clues from what I read and embellish his other-world characters to match. But he simply didn't relate the other world to this one.

For example, he had said the man he met on the half shell spoke in French and Latin and telepathy. I didn't know until I looked it up later that Nostradamus thought in Latin and wrote in French. When I pointed this out to Peter he merely shrugged and said, "Ya, but the man with the beard on the half shell also spoke with telepathy."

"Did this man also tell you he was a healer?" I asked.

"No. He just said he makes prophecies, sees into the future. And the past."

"When he told you that you would have this gift, did he say how? Did he say you would have it from touching objects, psychometry?"

"No. Nothing specific like that. Nobody up there told me specific how I do my gift. They just say I will see through things, and I have strong hands and fingers. That's why I paint, play the organ, feel the objects."

"Let me tell you something," said Tess. "Peter really has some strange power in his fingers. I know. Once I had something wrong with my shoulder and it was very painful, so Peter took off his rings and wristwatch and pressed my shoulder with those big fingers. . . . They were like hot burning fire, but the pain went away. I don't how he does it."

"It's the battery from my body," Peter explained. "From the other world."

"I think Peter has a power for diagnosing and healing people that could be just as strong as Edgar Cayce's if he wanted to use it that way. He is almost always 100 per cent right when he's telling people what's wrong with them . . . or anything that has to do with a physical ailment. I've seen it, I know," said Tess.

Although he has never claimed to be a psychic diagnostician or healer, as Edgar Cayce was, Peter's gift often seems to lend itself in that direction. Even Lynn Cayce, brother of the famed psychic, once told me that he was astonished at Peter's accuracy in medical matters.

Where does it come from?

"Up there," is all Peter can tell you.

Tess asked, "Do you know about Peter's death sweats?"

"Death sweats?" No, I didn't know.

"That's why I don't like cemeteries," said Peter. "Too many vibrations from the dead."

"But this is more than vibrations, Peter. Remember when you got the whiplashes?"

"Yes. Yes. I lived the man's life again. I don't want to think about it now." He walked out of the room.

Tess went on, "Peter was doing his show one night in Syracuse, dressed in his beautiful tuxedo and shirt, and a woman came up onstage and gave him a picture of a man, and asked Peter to tell her what he saw.

"Peter told her he saw the man in a concentration camp and he was being whipped and tortured. The woman started crying. She said that was her brother. Ordinarily Peter doesn't tell people things like this, but sometimes he can't help himself. I looked at him and all of a sudden I saw that his face was completely white, there was no color in it at all, and I thought he was going to pass out. We took him off the stage and into the kitchen and sat him down. Stephy gave him a Valium and blew up a bag and told him to breathe from it to get oxygen. It was as though he had forgotten to breathe for himself, as though he had just left his body.

"But that wasn't all. My brother Dom was there, and he went to loosen Peter's tie and coat, and I heard him say, 'What's that on your shirt?' There were red stains on the shirt, and when we looked closely we saw that Peter was bleeding. He was bleeding right through his shirt! We were all there. We saw it. Then we opened his shirt and we saw that he had these whiplashes on his body."

I said, "Excuse me, please, but I think you are plain nuts. Cuckoo. Like Peter."

"Well," Tess continued calmly, "there happened to be a doctor in the audience. He came and looked at Peter. He saw the whip marks but he said he couldn't understand how they got there.

"All I know is that we were all there and we all saw it. You could find fifteen witnesses who were there and saw it. And the next day Peter was so sick that he couldn't work. His chest hurt and he was in great pain. But by that night all the marks were gone. The only way I can explain it is that Peter is a sensitive and when he picked up from this man who had been in the concentration camp, he just suddenly started to live the life of that man, and that's why the whiplash marks appeared on his body."

There was no doubt that both Tess and Stephy really thought they had seen blood on Peter's shirt and whip marks on his chest. And Peter, of course, had seen them too—and felt them.

"Sure, I could feel them and they hurt like hell. I was reliving the life of that man in the concentration camp," he said.

Although fifteen witnesses or even fifteen million couldn't prove it, this is actually a type of psychic phenomena that has been recorded not only in the literature of the occult but even in such trusty bibles of research as The Columbia Encyclopedia. It comes under the heading of *stigmata.*

> STIGMATA . . . the plural of stigma (from the Greek) meaning brand. . . . St. Francis of Assisi, according to contemporary biographers, had in his later life wounds in his hands, his feet, and his sides, which bled profusely and were intensely painful. They had no mechanical or apparent cause, but were thought to be reproductions of the wounds of Jesus in his passion. Since then, some 300 Roman Catholics (all but 40 being women) have allegedly received similar wounds or stigmata, the existence of most of them being fully attested. Some of the 29 cases of the stigmata in the 19th century were carefully investigated by physicians, who were convinced of their objective reality and of the honesty of the stigmatized. This is also true of Theresa Neumann (of Konnersreuth, Upper Palatinate, Germany), first stigmatized in 1926. The phenomena of stigmatization have been studied but not adequately explained by non-Catholic scientists; they generally incline to believe the stigmata to be connected with nervous or cataleptic hysteria.

Peter, of course, had never heard of stigmata. When I read this to him, he listened attentively, then asked, "What is cataleptic?"

I read to him from a dictionary:

> CATALEPSY . . . (Greek katalepsis, a seizing). A condition of muscle rigidity and sudden, temporary loss of consciousness, as in epilepsy. . . .

"Well, Peter, it looks as though you came back with some rather peculiar gifts from up there," I said lightly.

He was not amused. "I am not in epilepsy and my wounds did not come from Jesus," he said hotly. "They came from the man in the concentration camp. I was living his life again, when they torture and whiplash him to death. Now, you see why I told the man in the half shell I don't want to see into the past? No good. I wish I would not have this gift. I wish I could switch it off."

"Was this the only time you ever had such an experience?" I asked.

"Yes. Only that one. But I feel death many, many times. My hand starts sweating like hell if I feel death, even through an envelope. It's the death sweat. And sometimes if I don't feel it right away, the Voice tells me there is death. . . ."

"Do you think the Voice belongs to the man in the half shell?"

"I don't know. All the same voice from the nine jurymen, like one voice. . . . It does not go away."

Between all the astral entities Peter encountered in the other world, it was obvious that he had come back to this one with some special gifts that were more burden than blessing.

To get his mind off his "death sweats," I brought him back to Nostradamus and some of his famous predictions.

"You said this was the man who told you that you would be working with the police on crime cases, right?"

"Ya, the man on the half shell and it upset me because I am frightened of the police."

"But he was right, wasn't he?"

"Sure. Okay. He was a good man but I don't want his gift."

"Listen to this, Peter, he was supposed to be pretty good at predicting. He predicted the French Revolution, the failure of the League of Nations, the Spanish Civil War, the abdication of Edward VIII . . . World War II . . . the D-day invasion. . . . He also predicted the Lindbergh kidnapping—"

"Are you kidding?" Peter interrupted. Until then he had been totally uninterested but the word "kidnapping" caught his attention. It brought him down to planet Earth and a case that was currently in the headlines, one that he had worked on briefly in the beginning. It was the Patty Hearst case.

About a week after Patty Hearst was kidnapped (on February 4, 1974), I was contacted by a member of the Hearst family who said that Mr. Randolph Hearst, Patty's father, wished to get in touch with Peter Hurkos. Could I arrange this?

I called Stephy, who relayed the message to Peter. Although

Peter doesn't like to talk on the phone, this time he came on and said, "You call him. Tell him I do not want to go to San Francisco. Too dangerous. They would kill the girl. Tell him if he wants to come here and see me, bring me a piece of the girl's clothing."

That was all.

I called Mr. Hearst and gave him Peter's message. The next day his other daughter arrived with some of Patty's personal belongings, including clothing she had worn.

Peter's psychic consultations are confidential, the same as a doctor-patient relationship, unless a release is authorized. All I can say here is that Peter had told me at the time of the kidnapping: "The girl was taken by underground people. . . . Very bad people. . . . But she went with them now and is living with them and she is hiding out because she does not want to come back. . . . She is like brainwashed . . . living with them on farms, like communal . . . underground. . . . And there will be shooting and death before they find her. . . . She is like an animal hiding out . . . because she is brainwashed now . . . can't come back. . . . Long time if they ever find her."

Peter's psychic "gift" has probably brought little comfort to the Hearst family.

But his clairvoyance was remarkable, considering that he "saw" the events—the "underground people," the "hiding out," the "shooting and death"—many weeks before the Symbionese Liberation "kidnappers" surfaced to the headlines.

Even more remarkable was his work on the Sharon Tate case, one of the most gruesome and highly publicized murder cases in criminal history.* But how could a bearded seer on a floating half shell, circa 1941, predict that Peter would be working on crime cases?

* An account of Peter's work on that case is given in the Appendix.

{13}

The Touch {Psychometry}

PETER'S GIFT OF PSYCHOMETRY HAS AMAZED EVERYONE WHO HAS witnessed it. He does not know which of his guides in the other world gave him this specific gift, the ability to know or "see" things merely by touching an object—or a person.

For that matter, he didn't even know the meaning of the word "psychometry" until I explained it to him.

In his own way he says simply, "I touch. Then I see the pictures and I hear the Voice."

Sometimes the collective Voice of his bearded guides up there would tell him, "You have very strong hands, great power in your fingers."

And, as Peter says, "It's true. I have much power in my fingers. That's why I always paint with my fingers. No brush. Why I can play music. In my head I hear the music from the other world and my fingers know where to go."

He doesn't always need to touch an object or a person to get his "visions" or hear the Voice. I have often seen him come up with remarkable psychic readings on people even when he is sitting across the room from them. Usually these are spontaneous flashes of insight.

But sometimes it requires prolonged periods of deep concentration and "finger power" on an object, and as mentioned previously, he often sleeps with the objects.

Even a dead girl's fingernails!

Tess told the story of this murder case which Peter worked on with police in Pennsylvania. He was in Philadelphia for an appearance on the Mike Douglas Show when police from another city contacted him.

"A beautiful young girl had been murdered—stabbed to death —and the police so far had no suspects, absolutely no clues or leads, nothing to go on, so they called Peter in," Tess said. "The girl's father was the one who suggested Peter. He was grief-stricken and desperately reaching for anything that would help find the murderer. He brought in pictures of the girl and several items of clothing and jewelry.

"Peter worked three or four nights and still couldn't get anything solid enough for them to go on. Of course, he could tell everything about the girl herself, her activities, her boy friends—but still no clues that would lead her to her murderer.

"Then her father came in with this little plastic bag, and there were these two fingernails from the dead girl's body and—"

"Wait a minute," I interrupted. "Do you mean that you actually saw the two fingernails—from the dead girl's body?"

"Sure. Oh, you get used to these things when you work with Peter," said Tess, obviously noticing the look of horror on my face.

"Well, I wouldn't," I said. "And that's why I don't like getting all those funny packages in the mail that people are always sending me for Peter."

Ever since *The Psychic World of Peter Hurkos* was published (1970), I have been besieged not only by letters and phone calls from all over the world (and at all hours of the day and night), but by many mysterious packages as well, from people who want Peter to psychometrize something for them. Please, dear readers, no more packages! They spook me.

Tess went on with her story about the fingernails.

"Well, I have never seen Peter do anything like this before. He took the fingernails out of the bag and held them in one hand, and with his other hand he began drawing. It was as though the pictures just came out of him automatically. First he drew a picture of a little old shack with an old trailer beside it, and then a path that led past a junkyard. All the time he was drawing the pictures he was talking, like to himself. It was exactly the same as what you read to us about Nostradamus—as though Peter were getting messages from somewhere while he was in a state of semisuspension of consciousness.

"The path he drew led to another house and there was a bar across the street . . . and there was another road leading to a schoolhouse. . . . Then, from his own reading of his own automatic drawing, he began giving a description of the boy . . . the area he lived in and where he went to school. . . . It gave me goose bumps as I watched and listened. And you should have seen the expression on the faces of those police officers and the girl's poor father.

"They obviously all recognized at least part of the area Peter was drawing, maybe the schoolhouse or the junkyard or the shack with the trailer beside it, I don't know. But when he got to the schoolhouse he started being more specific. The boy was very young, maybe fifteen or sixteen, still in school, and a good student, he said. He wrote nice letters to his teachers. But at night he was a Peeping Tom. He had seen the beautiful young girl through her window often. . . . He wanted to rape her. . . ."

Tess said the police had not suspected a schoolboy, because the killing seemed to have been done with so much strength and brutality.

"But that's exactly who it turned out to be, the schoolboy Peter described," Tess said. And he got the description from his own reading of his own picture while he was still drawing and while he was holding the girl's fingernails in his hand."

Peter doesn't especially enjoy psychometrizing objects quite so personalized, but he admits that they usually work best for him.

I have seen so many of Peter's fingertip readings through the years, and especially during our work on this book, that I should no longer be surprised at anything he comes up with. But occasionally I am so startled that I stupidly forget I'm dealing with a psychic.

This happened recently when we were about to start one of our other-world sessions.

In my mail that morning I had received another one of those letters (forwarded from Doubleday), this one from a man in Iowa who implored me to obtain for him a psychic reading from Peter. As usual he had a "problem" which he could not divulge to me, but he enclosed a picture of himself—a blond young man playing a guitar. He also considerately enclosed a check for five dollars made out to me—"for your trouble on my behalf." He said he didn't know what Peter's fee would be (it varies with each case) but he couldn't "afford very much."

(IMPORTANT TO READERS: I do NOT—repeat do NOT —accept money for putting anyone in contact with Peter Hurkos. So save yourselves the bother and me the bother of sending it back!)

The printed name on the check was a woman's name, and the name with return address on the upper left-hand corner of the envelope was also a woman's name. But the signature on the letter was a man's name, and the photograph looked like a man, although these days you never know.

I thought it might be interesting, before returning the five-dollar check, to have Peter psychometrize the envelope. The photo and check, folded in half with the written side in, were tucked between the triple fold of the letter.

Casually, I pushed the small envelope over to Peter. "Do you mind just a little warm-up before we get down to work?"

He fingered the envelope—but not for long.

"Can't tell if it's man or woman. . . . Yes, I know. . . . Man with woman problems."

He stopped, quickly tapped his fingertips on the envelope again, then tossed the envelope over to me in disgust, saying, "Tell the man if he wants consultation from me, don't send five dollars only. Five dollars! For this man I charge five hundred. And he can afford it. People like this I have nothing to do with. Cheap! Five dollars," he grumbled.

I was frankly dumfounded.

I opened the envelope, took out the picture and check, and showed them to Stephy, Tess, and Peter. He wouldn't even look at them.

"But I only got this in the mail today! How did you know about the check, Peter?"

"Oh, I just go over to your apartment and steal it from your mailbox. Right?"

He gave me a scathing look and walked out of the room.

"You've hurt his feelings," Stephy said quietly.

I already knew that.

"But how can he be so accurate? How could he see the check there? How did he know it was for five dollars instead of twenty-five?"

Stephy reminded me, with a hint of sarcasm, "Peter is psychic, you know."

Tess appraised me with her big brown eyes in which there was a faint hint of silent reprimand. But she politely held her tongue.

Obviously I had committed a terrible faux pas in asking Peter how he knew about the check.

Peter isn't a magician. He doesn't know the magician's tricks of the trade, among which one of the most common is "reading" sealed envelopes. He employs no gimmicks and is not a fakir.

Whatever gift he has is genuine. In retrospect, I can only believe that he knew about the check through psychometry—or telepathy. And possibly a combination of both.

Even as I write this I am still turning up pages from our original transcripts that are as incredible to me as they must be to readers.

In one of our early sessions I gave Peter a large envelope to psychometrize. Inside was another large orange folder, and inside that was a seven-page, single-spaced typed letter from a woman in Wisconsin, plus an eight-by-ten photo of a woman with a dog, and another envelope marked "Lalle's Coat Hair." I had not opened that one. But I had read the woman's heartbreaking letter and was sad as I looked at the photographs of the beautiful Old English prize-winning sheep dog who had mysteriously died or disappeared on his way to a dog show in Michigan.

As this is written, the case is still in litigation, so the names and places and some of the circumstances are changed. But the essential elements are still the same as far as Peter's role is concerned.

The woman—we'll call her Mrs. X—had bought and imported the lovely OES puppy from one of the finest breeding kennels in Europe and had groomed him as a show dog. He came from a long lineage of OES champions.

She had been showing him for only about six weeks when she was persuaded to send him with his handler to a weekend dog show in Michigan. It was his first trip away from home without her. (She couldn't go because of her job.) As he was loaded onto the van with the other dogs, she gave him a hug and a kiss and told him to bring home only the purple ribbons. That was the last time she saw Lalle.

She received a telephone call that Lalle had died suddenly. She requested that his body be shipped home. For some reason it was not. She asked for a post-mortem report from the veterinarian . . . and because of many discrepancies in the stories of various people involved she suspected foul play. She thought her dog had either been stolen or sold to someone who knew its value (approximately $10,000 for his "genetic stability") and another dog substituted in the vet's crematory.

Her letter was explicit in all its details, including persons she suspected of switching another dog's body for Lalle's. Peter had no possible way of knowing any of this when I gave him the big closed folder to psychometrize, with all its contents inside. *How* could he even know that he was psychometrizing a dog instead of a person?

Yet, here it is from the transcript, verbatim:

"Bleeding, I see bleeding. . . . He is kidnapped, run away, and the woman is crying. . . . I see the bleeding, then I see a death. It has to do with animals, and the woman is crying. . . . I see an accident on the road, the rips through his lungs. . . . It is a long-haired baby. . . . I mean like a baby, like a child but it's not a child. . . . It is an animal, young . . . and the woman is crying because the animal is dead. . . . Strange . . . I hear another language . . . it has to do with Scottish or Irish, but I don't understand this. . . .

"I see long hair . . . can't see the face . . . long hair . . . silver gray . . . and the woman is crying. . . . Dog is run away . . . then kidnapped. . . ."

Obviously what Peter saw—the long-haired baby-child-animal— was the young dog, three years old, whose photographs show him to have so much hair that you could not see his face. And he had picked up the "woman crying" from her letter. It was strange that he also picked up another language—"has to do with Scottish or Irish"—because much of the letter from Mrs. X dealt with her dog's Scottish-Swedish background . . . and he had arrived here on St. Patrick's Day.

Mrs. X thought her dog was stolen. Peter used the word "kidnapped." Most of these details, including the accident and death of the dog, which Mrs. X questioned at great length in her letter, might have been obtained by Peter through telepathy—from my mind, because I knew the contents of the letter. There was no other way he could know them.

He might also know by telepathy, because I had seen the pictures of the dog, that he was long-haired, with the hair covering his face.

But Mrs. X did not mention the color of the dog's hair, and I couldn't tell from the pictures. Only when I started to write this, checking the transcript and the Mrs. X folder, could I bring myself to open the envelope that had remained sealed for two years, the one on which she had written "Lalle's Coat Hair." Peter had called it "long hair . . . silver gray."

I forced myself to look inside the envelope, and there it was, a big, flattened sample of Lalle's long hair . . . silver gray.

Dogs come in many colors. Why didn't Peter guess him to be a brown-haired poodle?

What he "saw" through that big thick folder on Mrs. X didn't bring Lalle back to his mistress but it may play a role in retribution.

A recent letter from Mrs. X reads:

. . . I would like you and Peter to know that based on his reading I went all out and sent an attorney to Michigan to get the depositions of the veterinarians involved. We now have positive proof that it was NOT Lalle's body that was delivered to the vets for post-mortem examination. . . .

I have signed the complaint and we should have the handler in court as soon as we can get a date. . . .

I just wanted you to know that with the information I have now, this proves Peter's accuracy, although I am still hoping that he is wrong on one point and that eventually I will find Lalle alive. . . .

Peter's gift of psychometry has become so second nature with him that he becomes easily bored—or annoyed—with people who are always thrusting objects, pictures, and sealed envelopes at him just for a casual reading. When he's working on an important case, that's different. Then he is psychometrizing at his best. But he resents being constantly tested by skeptics who merely want him to prove his gift, who would laugh if he told them it came from the other world, and who suspiciously regard him as a pseudo-psychic charlatan. This isn't surprising, however, when you consider the origin of psychometry.

Psychometry has a fascinating history. It is believed that the word "psychometry" was first applied by the ancient Egyptians to the weighing of souls. The notion of a personal influence clinging to an object, for good or ill, and carrying a reminiscence of a fate recurs in many a myth and tradition.

But the dubious honor of developing the practice of psychometry as a commercial art or pseudo-science rests with one Joseph Rhodes Buchanan, an anthropologist and self-appointed "professor" in several medical schools of the eclectic variety. He claims to have discovered psychometry in 1842 in New York, and his "discovery" was formally announced in 1849 in Cincinnati in Buchanan's *Journal of Man*.

Buchanan and his wife gave "psychometric readings" to all comers at two dollars each, and "elaborate opinions" at five dollars.

Their method was to place an object upon the forehead of a "sensitive," who would close his eyes and concentrate until he received images and the "peculiar influence" of the person associated with the object.

The psychometrizing of autographs became a popular psychic indoor sport among Dr. Buchanan's followers. Later, the psychometry cult turned to geology. A rock fossil was placed upon the head of a "sensitive," and lo and behold, it would arouse a full description of the state of the earth eons back, when the specimen was formed.

In his fascinating book *Error and Eccentricity in Human Belief* (Dover, 1935), American psychologist Joseph Jastrow, a master debunker of myths, magic, and mystical vagaries, puts psychometry in the category of just "another psychic folly" for dupes and victims of self-delusion. He attributes the popularity of such "wayward beliefs" primarily to credulity, the human urge to believe, especially in the supernatural, and the notion that the dead still live and the past continues. "The prepossessed mind finds what it looks for," he wrote.

It is unquestionably true that psychometry, like other forms of psychic phenomena, has been exploited, misused, and abused by fakers and fringe "psychic" con artists.

This does not, however, eliminate the empirical evidence that through the ages many people have personally experienced many forms of genuine psychic phenomena, and that some persons are more acutely sensitive in this area than others.

Since Jastrow's book was written, in 1935, a great deal of scientific research has been going on (though much more needs to be done) with various types of psychic phenomena, including psychometry. The experimental work done by Dr. Eugene Osty, a French physician with a scientific approach to psychical research, has established the phenomenon of psychometry with a very high degree of probability, and also revealed some of the conditions under which it takes place.

Dr. Osty became director of the Institut Metapsychique International in Paris and for many years made investigations of a group of talented French sensitives. His contributions to the study of psychometry are among the most important in psychic literature. He tested some sensitives while they were under hypnosis, others in a waking state, always using an object that had been in contact with a person.

It was his conclusion that the so-called paranormal knowledge of the sensitive was derived from the subject, i.e., the person who had once touched the object. Some of his subjects, he revealed, were able to establish rapport on a deeper or "transcendental plane" and at times appeared to have foreknowledge of the future.

There is one hypothesis that all objects have a kind of lingering aura, sometimes called a "psychic ether."

Dr. F. Regis Riesenman calls it an "odic force." It is his theory that a murderer, for example, leaves a trail of emotion—anger, fear, resentment, appendages of the crime—that a psychic can latch onto even years after the incident. This odic force supposedly clings to a person's clothing or other personal possessions. "This is why Peter is so fantastically great on criminal cases. He can pick up all of these impressions through the odic force," Dr. Riesenmann explains.

By whatever name it is called, "psychic ether," "aura," "odic force," or "vibrations," there is now evidence that the fingertips— at least some people's fingertips—are sensitive enough to pick up *something* that enables a person to "read" or "see" by psychometry or what is sometimes called "fingertip reading." Any blind person who reads by Braille doesn't need to be told about the acute sensitivity of the fingertips. But in recent years, research in fingertip reading, particularly in Russia but also in France and America, and with both the blind and nonblind, has fairly well established it as a genuine phenomenon.

In the early 1960s, a twenty-two-year-old Russian girl, Rosa Kuleshova, startled the world with her fingertip reading. The blind girl was brought from her Ural Mountain home to Moscow to be examined in the laboratories of the Soviet Academy of Sciences. Her ability to "see" with her fingertips was certified as genuine by Soviet scientists, and she emerged a celebrity.

The Soviets proclaimed it the "Rosa Kuleshova Phenomenon." The French, in their own experiments, referred to it as "paraoptic ability." American researchers call it "eyeless sight" or "dermo-optics."

There have been many experiments with art students, blind, nonblind, and blindfolded, who were able to perceive colors accurately through their fingertips.

Dr. Gregory Razran, head of the psychology department of Queens College in New York, and an expert on Soviet psychology for the National Institutes of Health, has stated, "It is, after all, the kind of thing one automatically disbelieves. But there is no longer any doubt in my mind that this work is valid."

Although the scientific community may not want to admit it, at least psychometry has made some progress since the days when the Egyptians were using it for the weighing of souls.

And for that matter, who knows but what this was where Peter learned it?

For he was there with them in the pyramids in one of the strangest of all his experiences on his out-of-body journey in the other world.

{14}

The Pyramids and
the Lost Atlantis

FOR CENTURIES, MEN HAVE TRIED TO PROBE THE MYSTERIES OF THE
Great Pyramids of Egypt. How were they built and by whom?
And for what purpose? Are there really hidden chambers that con-
tain secrets of the universe, as many have claimed?

The Great Pyramids remain one of the seven wonders of the
world and one of the strangest works of architecture in existence.
And to this day scientists with sonar and radar equipment are trying to detect signs of secret chambers or passageways either within
or underground between the pyramids. So far modern technology
has failed to find answers to the many puzzles still surrounding the
pyramids.

In nonscientific circles and especially among occultists there has
long been a popular belief that the pyramids were built by extra-

terrestial beings from another planet. No sign of the builders has ever been found. They seem to have vanished from the face of the earth as mysteriously as they appeared.

More recently there has developed a widespread interest in so-called pyramid power, the theory being that there is an "energy force" inside the pyramidal form that can sharpen razor blades, mummify eggs, and improve sexual sensitivity.

Some people speculate that the pyramidal form may be some gigantic lens that is able to focus an unknown energy by its shape; and the hypothesis is that experiments with small-model pyramids offer evidence of advanced energy systems within the Great Pyramids.

Peter doesn't know anything about "pyramid power," but from the beginning I had noticed how often he described the light, both the hot light that sucked him up into the other world and the one that seemed to be everywhere up there, as a "pyramid" light, or a triangle, and how he sometimes referred to it as an "energy source."

Now he was about to take us on a strange journey within the Great Pyramids—and until science unlocks their secrets, if it ever does, who can disprove what he saw there?

He was walking alone in the mountains one day when he saw the pyramid of light that always seemed to be shining from somewhere. This time it was brighter than usual. He was puzzled about where it came from. What was it source? He began walking toward it, faster and faster.

"It seemed like I was walking for miles but I was not tired from the walking because it was more like I was walking on feathers."

He was coming closer and closer to the light when suddenly he stopped, transfixed in wonder.

"At first I thought it was just a vision, that I was seeing things that weren't there. And I had this strong feeling that I have been here before."

The "vision" he saw was the Great Pyramids of Egypt. They were exactly as he had seen them in pictures, and as he had seen them when he was a sailor—but from a distance.

Peter had left home when he was fourteen and run away to sea.

He had signed on his first ship as a cook's assistant, the youngest member of the crew. But he looked eighteen. He was almost six feet tall even then. He had broad shoulders and black curly hair and was growing into a handsome young man. The sea not only gave him a sense of peacefulness but it introduced him to the wonders of faraway places, and one of his earliest memories from those seafaring days was his first glimpse of the Great Pyramids.

"I will never forget it. Never. We were going up the Suez Canal, I think we were about halfway through it, and the other sailors said, 'Hey, kid, come and look,' and there they were, the Great Pyramids. They were about thirty miles away but so plain and like nothing I ever saw in this world again. They looked like they were from some other world. I heard sailors talk about the secret tunnels and chambers, and I said, someday I am going to come back here and go into those pyramids and find the secrets. But I never did, not in this world. Only in that other world," he said.

Peter was disturbed at the vision. He had left all remnants of his earthly life behind. There was not even the memory of his dog, Tommy, to haunt him. But now, out of the past, appeared the pyramids he had seen once, long before his fall.

And as mysteriously as the pyramids materialized out of nowhere, so did a shadowy figure who appeared at his side and said, "You have these also in the world you come from, but no one knows their secret. Would you like to come with me? I'll show you."

"Who are you?" Peter asked.

"I am your guide. Come."

"Did you recognize him?" I asked.

"I don't know. I think he was one of the jurymen but I am so confused now," Peter said. "He was not the composer but I could hear music around him, a different kind of music. Strange. He put me on a platform and we started going down, down. . . ."

"What kind of platform did you go down on, Peter?"

"Half shell. That is all their transportation up there. The half shell is what you might call a flying object but not quite. It isn't flying, it is more like floating, and it is shaped like half a shell from an oyster. No engine, no noise. People there are much more advanced in transportation. The platform we went on was still a half shell but bigger and it could go right through the walls and the chambers and the tunnels and the canals. And it could go up and down underground, on many levels," Peter explained.

"Where did your guide take you first?"

"Through the tunnels that connect the three pyramids. They were wide and dark, with many shadows and strange smells. But I could feel the energy in them, strong energy, and I could still see the light at the top, though we were underground.

"Then we were inside the big pyramid, and on the walls everywhere there was a strange writing—numbers and symbols and pictures. . . ."

"Hieroglyphics," I said.

"What you mean hieroglyphics?"

I read the definition to him: HIEROGLYPHIC: A sacred character in the picture writing of the ancient Egyptians, etc. Derived from the Greek *hieroglyphikos,* meaning sacred (hieros) and to carve (glyphein).

"Okay, what the man showed me was symbolic writing and numbers and pictures, many animals. [Many animals were sacred to the ancient Egyptians.] He told me that everything is written here in the pyramids, everything in the whole world, everything that has happened and things that will happen in the future . . . like prophecies. . . . He also told me everything that is written up there in the pyramids is also written down here in the pyramids in Egypt. . . . But it is not translated yet. . . ."

"Did you ask him if it would ever be translated?"

"Yes. He told me someday it would be translated but only by people on a higher plane. Then I asked him, please, sir, would he tell me who built the pyramids and how they were built.

"He said to me, 'I know who you are and why you are here. And I know that you are going to be sent back to your world with a gift. But while you are here, you are on a higher plane and we trust you with many of our secrets because you are beginning to have understanding. When you go back, people will laugh at you.

Do you still want to know how your Great Pyramids of Egypt were built?'

"Yes. Definite. I want to know," Peter told him.

The shadowy figure on the half-shell platform told him, "They were built by the people from here and from another world. The people came down to earth and gave the knowledge to the Egyptians. The secret will be found someday. It is locked up, in a sealed chamber."

"Wait a minute, Peter," I interrupted. "This is a little far-out. You mean the people up there in that other world were the ones who came down here and told the Egyptians how to build the pyramids?"

"Yes. Definite. These people who did the building on the pyramids, they were much further in civilization than the people here on earth. They had much more knowledge than the Egyptians."

"The guide mentioned another world. Did he mean another one besides the one you were in?"

"Yes. Another world or planet or something, I don't know. But he said there were many people, like souls or spirit people, who came to Egypt, like a big migration, and they teach the Egyptians how to build the pyramids. They are much older than the Egyptians and know already a higher civilization. And the man told me many of those people are up there in the other world, and some are down here on earth but in different lives. And some are still there in a big city under the pyramids. . . ."

"Did he show you the city?"

"Yes. Sure," Peter said impatiently. "But let me tell you something else what happened first. We went out of the half shell and he showed me the secret of how the pyramids were built, with the water and the energy from the light . . . same as in the other world where I was. . . . The people who built the pyramids used power, not machinery. . . . The energy from the water made the ton of stone just like five kilos. That's how the pyramids were put up. The reason they didn't use cement or anything is that when the rock was wet, it was light. When it dried out, it was solid rock. [Apparently the same process he had described earlier.]

And you know those stones were not found in Egypt. They were found far, far away. And the people used the fluid, the secret of gravity from the other world. . . . And it was those people who wrote the inscriptions with the history of the world in the pyramids. . . . They have also built statues, symbolic statues all over the world. . . . They used them as signs, as a kind of compass. . . . The pyramids were not built by the Egyptians. They were built by psychic people who did not have to use machinery or cement, they used the energy power from the water and the light. . . . It is all there in the symbolic writing, the records they left in the secret chamber, all sealed up."

The guide took him through many chambers, showed him stores of jewels and treasures from the Pharaohs, and strange circular stones, metals, altars, and temples that seemed to be from a different civilization.

"Did you see any other people in the pyramids up there?" I asked Peter.

"Oh, yes, many people. But they were different. All very old."

"Pharaohs?"

"Yes, Pharaohs."

"Did you see the mummies?"

"Yes. But later. In the museum in New York. In the pyramids I saw mummies but they were—not dead. Like souls. Alive."

I couldn't resist asking, "Did you see anyone weighing in the souls?"

"What do you mean, weighing souls? You think I'm crazy?"

I explained to him about the origin of the word psychometry as being applied to the ancient Egyptians and their "weighing of souls" to determine the personal influence clinging to a body or an object. He didn't understand and was unimpressed.

"But I tell you one thing," he said. "I remember the smell, how strong the odor from the perfume and incense and I saw how they balsam [meaning embalm] the bodies and put them in the tomb. I remember all the number-symbols and meters I saw there and the strange music like in numbers, too. I ask my guide, what kind of music is this, and he said, when you go back you will understand. So now I play the music where my hands go. . . ."

In the jumble of sensory impressions he felt in the pyramids there were three that apparently affected him the most: the odors (smell), the music (sound), and the "number-symbols" (visual), as he calls them.

"Did the guide ever take you to the hidden chamber, the locked room with all the secrets of the pyramid builders?" I asked.

"Yes, yes. I am coming to that. It was in the middle where the tunnels are connecting the three pyramids. We go down, down again and then we come to a big chamber, all stone, sealed shut, number-symbols carved all over.

"The man said to me, 'This is where we keep the secret records from the people who have built the pyramids. It is the same hidden chamber you have in your Great Pyramids of Egypt, but the secret has not been found yet. If I let you see it, you must promise me one thing—that when you go back to your world you will take your people a message of understanding. You will tell them what you saw here and how your pyramids were built by people from another world. Come. I show you the records.' . . . Then he took a big key from somewhere—I don't know where he got it but he unlocked the big door and it came open easy, and we went in."

Inside, laid out on great stone tables, were big rough stones much like those used in building the pyramids but all carved with pictures, geometric designs, and the number-symbols, which Peter could not decipher.

"These are the records from the pyramid builders," the guide told him. "They tell the story of the great migration of spirit people to Egypt to build the pyramids and improve the race of people. And what is going to happen in your world is written in these stones."

"Where did these people come from?" Peter asked.

"Come, I show you," the man said.

They left the great stone record room and the half-shell platform started a swift descent down, down, down. . . .

"Right in the middle, underneath the sealed chamber, all underground from the big pyramid," Peter explained. "We go down, down, deep down, so fast all I could see was the light . . . orange up above and blue below . . . blue like water. . . ."

And as they went down, down, I knew what Peter was going to say next. Still, I couldn't believe it when he said it.

"So we go down so fast and then I see a completely other city underground. There were many canals and we went up and down the canals and we saw all the gardens and the beautiful factories for making food and plants from the light. I ask why is this, the factories underground for food, and he told me there is too much light above for what they are growing here, the plants grow much better here below. He said it grows from the light and the energy. . . . It is a whole city I see underground, buried under the pyramids. And the people are different. Not Egyptians. These are the people who built the pyramids and then leave the stones with the symbols . . . people from another planet. I don't know where. . . ."

"Did you talk to the people, Peter?"

"No. They talk only by telepathy. Very psychic. Very high intellectual. Very far in civilization, even before the Egyptians. And they have the secret buried with them, under the city."

"I thought you said their secrets were all in that sealed record chamber."

"No, no. Much more important. There is buried energy here that can light a whole world. You see, there is a whole city here buried under the pyramids, but where the city is you go down, down again below, underground, and that's where the energy is . . . the big energy plant from the light. . . ."

"You seem very sure of this, Peter. How can you be so sure? Did you go down to the energy plant?"

"No, no, no! Only the people there in the city under the pyramids know how to work the energy plant. But the man with the beard, the man with me on the platform told me when we went down to the city. He said, 'There is a buried energy under here that can light up a whole world.' He pointed it out to me: 'Look, you can see it everywhere, we cut the energy in three angles and it lights up.' I told him the pyramids we have down here have no light, and he said the reason is that this is sealed and it's never found. But the energy plant is in the pyramids down here, same as up there . . . both underground . . . down, down below the city. . . .

"It's the ray of light from the center that can light up the whole world. And the city up there is lighted from three-angle pyramids," Peter explained. He drew sketches to illustrate.

"Here, outside the pyramids, is where they have found the graves that were stolen from by body stealers, but they have never found the source of the energy, the light. And the reason is, we have found out too many things about light and energy, but dangerous things like explosion and bombs. Where I was they use light for good purpose only. We use it for killing each other. With what we have found out, we could use the energy power for good purposes, but we are destroying ourselves. And we could destroy the whole world. That's why the people under the pyramids keep their energy plant secret," Peter said.

Maybe I was letting my imagination run away with me, but throughout Peter's report on his journey into the pyramids, especially his guide's revelations about a "migration of spirit people" to Egypt who were more highly civilized and enlightened than the Egyptians, as well as his visit to the sealed record chamber and the city of non-Egyptian migratory souls below, I had been inwardly stirred by a vague recollection of Edgar Cayce's theories on the legendary lost Atlantis.

I didn't remember it well enough then for Peter to be receiving clues by telepathy.

But I went home and looked up my Edgar Cayce "life readings" on Atlantis. If Peter was far-out, Cayce was even more so. His psychic knowledge of Atlantis and the Atlanteans was acquired during one of his previous incarnations—as Priest Ra-Ta, leader of a Carpathian tribe that invaded and conquered Egypt at about the time the Atlanteans landed there after the destruction of their island continent.

In Egypt, Ra-Ta's religious teachings attracted a large following, and between Ra-Ta and the migrations of Atlanteans, a far superior race of people (says Cayce), there ensued a period of great advancement in the human race. It was Priest Ra-Ta who correlated all the Atlanteans' activities, the great exodus to Egypt, the building of temples and pyramids, the dissemination of knowledge to the Egyptians (in chemistry, building, economics, commerce, labor, the arts and music), and the transport of all their records from Atlantis to Egypt to be preserved in a sealed room in the pyramids.

Cayce called it the "Hall of Records." He said the secrets of the pyramids are written in the language of mathematics, geometry, and astronomy as well as in the symbology of the kinds of stone used, and he maintained that for those who could read it the Great Pyramid was a record in stone of the history and development of man from earliest times to 1998.

He also said that the secrets which the Atlanteans carried to Egypt are housed in a *still undiscovered* pyramid—and apparently he should know since he was there.

When I relayed all of this to Peter, his response was, "That Priest Ra-Ta must have been quite a guy. I wish I had met him but I didn't."

"You have heard about the lost Atlantis?" I asked.

"Sure. Big island. Like a mushroom. Mushroom broke and it came down. Fault from nature. Same will happen to Curaçao and other islands like mushrooms which will go under. The pressure of the water is taking away some of the bottom," he said matter-of-factly.

"Do you know where Atlantis was located?"

"In the Mediterranean. By Greece, I think."

"Do you think it was the people from Atlantis who brought the stone records to the pyramids?"

"How could they? The mushroom go down. All the people, too."

Edgar Cayce had said that the lost continent of Atlantis would rise again somewhere in the Atlantic Ocean. Maybe his geography was off. Could it be that the city Peter saw under the pyramids was Atlantis? It was an intriguing speculation. But Peter wouldn't go along with it.

"No," he said, "they were people from another planet, not a mushroom island that went under."

As for Edgar Cayce's life readings on Atlantis from his previous incarnation as Priest Ra-Ta, Peter's response was—from one psychic to another—"Phoney baloney! I don't get my information like that. I get it from the people in the other world."

When I asked Peter if he had ever heard of something called pyramid power, he exploded, "Oh my God! What do you think I have been talking about all this time?"

I explained to him about the current interest in the geometric shape of the pyramids and the theory that it generates an "energy force" that supposedly can sharpen razor blades, preserve foodstuffs, improve sexual sensitivity, and make better mummies.

"Oh, yes?" He expressed mild curiosity, then laughed. "I don't need it for sexual anything."

But at least there is a glimmer of scientific interest in the current fad. It has been reliably reported that several NASA scientists have been doing "pyramid energy" experiments in their basements at night. One was quoted as saying, "This is scientifically impossible. Call it what you will—occultism, the curse of the pharaohs, sorcery, or magic—there is some force that defies the laws of science at work in the pyramid."

Peter had mentioned seeing some mummies in a museum in New York. I asked him to elaborate on this.

"It was when I first came to this country in 1956. Someone took me to a museum in New York. I do not know its name. I had never been in a museum before.

"They took me to the area where the mummies were, and then I became all confused, almost blacked out. I was cold and sweating. . . . I was in another world . . . like thousands of years ago. . . . I smelled the perfume. . . . I saw how they balsam the bodies and put them in the tomb. . . . One of the coffins I saw in the museum was open and the other one was closed. . . . But I saw the inscriptions and the symbolic drawings, same as I saw in the pyramids in the other world. . . . I saw how they build the pyramids by cutting the stones with the light and using the water for weightlessness. . . .

"Then I was so frightened and confused that I ran out of the museum and I couldn't even find my own car or the hotel where I was staying . . . I was in so deep with the mummies . . . I felt so much heavy. . . . Then I had a tremendous headache and I blacked out. . . . They take me back to my hotel and I couldn't sleep. . . . I was the whole night in Egypt . . . the whole night and the next day. . . . I couldn't see anything else, but not because I was blind . . . because of my mind. . . . I went too deep in . . . so many years back . . . and they tell me I use funny words that I don't know. . . ."

"Did this ever happen to you at any other time?"

"Oh, yes, it happens all the time, but not so bad as with the mummies. But many times when I play music, when I paint, I go back to that time when the people lived. But that is a peaceful time. Not like with the mummies. When we went to Paris, Stephy took me to see the 'Mona Lisa.' I didn't want to go to museum again. I didn't want to stay too long in there. I go too deep in. . . ."

I had one more question to ask Peter. During his entire description of his journey through the pyramids I had been puzzled by his continual reference to the number-symbols and the strange music he heard inside the pyramids—different from that outside. The number-symbols alone were not significant, as the Egyptian hieroglyphics included mystical numbers, as well as animals, elements, and gods (especially the sun god Ra) in their symbology. But Peter had said one of the nine men on his jury was a mathematician, and his association of numbers and music with the guide who took him through the pyramids led me to some library diggings. I knew little, if any, more about mathematics and mathematicians than Peter did, except that music is in some way related to mathematics.

I finally ran across a clue in a treatise on pyramid power by Max Toth, the razor-blade-sharpening man, president of the Toth Pyramid Co., an expert in the occult and a knowledgeable Egyptologist. In an article, "The Mysterious Pyramids" (published in *Beyond Reality*, December 1972), he wrote:

> . . . more technically may be mentioned the Egyptian belief that each of the basic geometric solids had therapeutic powers. Forms, designs, arrangements, and patterns, capture and hold energy. In fact, the extension of the Pythagorean formula shows that if man can produce or construct a completely perfect form, it will convey back to him through his sensory perceptions, a powerful energy for the restoration of his own normalcy.

I had a strong suspicion that the Pythagorean formula had something to do with why I almost flunked mathematics. I certainly didn't know that Pythagoras had anything to do with the pyramids. I still don't. But when I checked up on him I found some intriguing anomalies.

Pythagoras was a Greek philosopher (582–507 B.C.) who is regarded as the founder and father of numerology. He believed that everything in the universe is expressed in numbers, and is credited with inspiring (in practical mathematics) the first part of Euclidean geometry and the Pythagorean theorem.

He also was a man of mystical inclination, and founded a religious cult that believed in the "transmigration of souls" and reincarnation. (Peter's guide had told him about "migration" of spirit people to Egypt.)

More important, as far as Peter is concerned, it was Pythagoras who made the startling discovery that musical tones have numerical interrelations, that musical intervals depend upon the simple relations of vibrations: 1 to 2 (octave), 2 to 3 (fifth), and 3 to 4 (third). For this and many another discovery he was regarded as a great pioneer in science.

Neither Peter nor I knew anything about the musical-numerical interrelations. But I was positive that Peter had psychically and subconsciously acquired enough knowledge of them from someone in the other world to make his hands know where to go on the organ and the piano.

Peter of course had never heard of Pythagoras. I gave him his picture to psychometrize and asked, "Would this happen to be the man who was your guide through the pyramids?"

He ran his fingertips over the picture and said, "Ya, ya, that's the guy. He was there, too, on the jury."

I explained that Pythagoras was a famous mathematician.

"But I'm not interested in mathematics," he said bluntly. "What has that got to do with music?"

{15}

The Verdict

THE TIME HAD COME FOR PETER TO RETURN TO THE DOMED MEETING hall for the verdict that was awaiting him.

How much time had elapsed between the first and second meetings, he doesn't know.

His hospital records show that he was unconscious four days.

But Peter says, "There is no time of the clock there, or the calendar. No Saturday or Sunday or Monday. It is the world of abstract, no time or space."

He remembers that his judgment day began much like the first day of his arrival in the other world, with the nine shadowy figures approaching from a distance, and their voices as one voice saying, "It is time now. Come."

Then they were inside the meeting hall, and as the bearded figures took their places in the marble chairs behind the long marble table, Peter became uncomfortably aware that the hall was filled with people. . . . It seemed to him like thousands of people, all shadowy and indistinct: "Just their faces and eyes, all staring at me." And in the background he could hear the celestial choir and the music, soft and sad and far away.

As he stepped before the jury he noticed again their white robes of filmy transparency, but this time he could not see through them as clearly as he had the first time.

He felt frightened and confused.

Then a voice from above spoke:

"The Master is here."

Peter looked up at the big marble chair on the platform above the jury table. It was still empty. He quickly looked from side to side, thinking the jurymen were awaiting the Master's arrival momentarily, but no one came to occupy the chair. He looked up and down the row of nine silent figures in front of him at the jury table. They were still the same, even the one at the far left end with the piercing eyes that he had recognized. But this time all the others had a look in their eyes that had not been there before. They were staring at him intently and their eyes were like sharp beams of light . . . electricity . . . "I could feel it going right through me," Peter recalls.

None of them spoke. Or at least Peter never once saw any of them open his mouth. Yet there was a voice that seemed to come from all of them at once . . . and always it came from the Big Master's marble chair up above them . . . the empty chair. Still Peter could see no one in it.

The far-off celestial music stopped. There was a long moment of complete silence, and then came the Voice, resounding like an echo from the domed marble walls, reverberating like a voice in a mausoleum.

"Peter the Fisherman!" the Voice rang out, like a bailiff calling a case in a courtroom.

Peter looked up, startled and shaken.

Peter the Fisherman was the name his mother had called him as a boy because he had loved the sea and he loved fishing. He could spend hours just sitting and staring at the sea and dreaming of the faraway places he would see someday. And many times he would skip school and go fishing in the canals of Dordrecht with his dog, Tommy. Often he would be late for his supper but he always came home with fish. His mother would scold him for being late, but then she would shake her head in resignation, muttering "My son, Peter the Fisherman, Peter the Fisherman."

No one else had ever called him that. He hadn't even thought of it himself for years. It had been a long time ago . . . when he had his dog, Tommy.

It all came back in a sharp, painful flash now, when the Voice called, "Peter the Fisherman!" Until then, everything had been so beautiful in that other world because Peter had no memory of anything in the life he had left behind. He did not remember his mother, he did not remember his dog, Tommy, he did not remember the sea or the canals or the fishing.

Why did the Voice have to remind him?

Now he could not shake the memories, and a strange feeling came over him.

"I felt like I was two people, like part of me was in two different worlds. I looked at all the jurymen and I felt like I was seeing double. They were all blurry, they would fade away and come back, and I screamed at them, 'How do you know I was Peter the Fisherman? I don't want to be Peter the Fisherman now. I want to stay here.' . . . I screamed at them, but nothing came out of my throat. . . ."

Peter was becoming more emotional as he talked. He was reliving the scene and the suffering. There was also the pain of realizing that they were about to send him back. . . .

The figures at the table in front of him remained silent and motionless, but he could feel the hot beams from their eyes as the Voice above them said, "You are a good man, Peter the Fisherman, but you are here by mistake. You are not ready to die yet. We cannot keep you here. We are sorry but we have to send you back."

"I do not want to go back to that darkness," Peter said.

"You will not have to go back to the darkness."

"I do not want to go back to that hell, that jail," Peter cried.

"Now, listen to me carefully," the Voice said. "We have no choice. We have to send you back, but when you go back you will not be the same Peter the Fisherman and you will not be a house painter. You will have a gift, many gifts from the souls you have met here but you must always use your gifts for good, never for evil."

"What kind of gift?" Peter asked.

"You will have to find out for yourself. Your gift will be in many different directions. And many times you will be lonely, you will be fighting alone because the people will not understand you, they will not believe you," the Voice said.

Peter bowed his head and began weeping in front of the jurymen. "I was crying deeply and pleading with them," he said.

The Voice said, "You must be strong, Peter. We will give you the energy to be strong. But you must believe. We will help you to believe but you must be strong. Hold your head up, Peter. . . . Hold out your hands, let us see your hands. . . ."

Peter raised his head and stretched his hands out toward the jurymen. For the first time the figures seemed to move or bend toward him with interest, instead of sitting motionless or fading in and out like an optical illusion. Peter remembers this scene as a kind of kaleidoscopic vision, a transfusion of reflected patterns and colors from the one big pyramid of light in the dome, as the figures floated forward and in and out looking intently at his hands. Now he could feel the beams of light from their eyes hot on his hands, tingling like an electric shock.

Then the Voice said, "You have strong hands and now you will have power in your hands. But you must use it only for good."

Peter asked, "Why did you bring me here and now you send me back?"

"We did not bring you here. You came by mistake," the Voice repeated. "But while you were here we showed you the light. You have learned many things and you will learn many more when you go back because we have a job for you to do."

"The only job I know is painting houses," Peter said.

"You will have a different kind of job with your gift."

"I don't want any gift. Maybe it will be a gift from the devil,"

Peter said. Suddenly the great domed hall shook with a tremor that would have registered five points on the Richter scale if it had been on planet Earth.

There was a long ominous silence. The bearded figures seemed to come to life. They looked at each other, shaking their heads. The beams of light in their eyes had switched off, and something curious had happened to the pyramid of light from above. It dimmed to an earthly triangle of fluorescent lights, then moved eerily across the domed ceiling to a spot just above the empty marble Master's chair. Slowly it came on again in brilliant luminescence—more luminous than ever. But its pyramid beams encompassed only the empty chair, with soft rays of light falling on the figures at the jury table.

Peter was aware that he had committed a sacred transgression. He stood abjectly awaiting his punishment.

He tried to penetrate through the blinding pyramid of light on the empty chair. Still he could see no one there.

But the Voice was there. Solemnly, in a ringing tone, it said, "Peter the Fisherman, you are on a higher, more noble plane now. We have shown you the light and still you speak of the devil. There is no devil here. You do not believe in God. You have no religion. You have never prayed and you are not a believer. Why don't you believe in God?"

Peter answered respectfully, "I didn't believe in God because I don't know who God is. . . . I wasn't brought up that way.

"My mother is Jewish and my father is Presbyterian. My father hated me to go to temple and we were not members. . . . And my mother did not want us to go to church. There was a friction between them. . . . I was never taught to be in a religion. . . . I knew there was something, but I didn't know what a God or a Jesus was."

Peter, sitting down here with us at the table with his Persian rug tablecloth, looked up and said, "I told this to the nine men, that I was never taught to be in a religion. Was I wrong? I don't know. But they knew anyway. They knew everything about me. . . . Then one of the men told me there is a God, but he wasn't there, he was on another planet, a higher planet, and I wondered why the God or the Jesus would not be sitting there in the chair. . . ."

The Voice took over again.

"Peter the Fisherman, you will never be called Peter the Fisherman again. Do you know who Peter the Fisherman is?"

"No."

"He is one of the first disciples that Jesus called, a carpenter and a fisherman, and when you go back to your world you cannot be called Peter the Fisherman but you will study the Bible and you will learn to believe what you have seen in this world. You will learn about Moses and why he was punished for his sin and forbidden to enter the Promised Land."

"But why am I being punished?" Peter asked. "Am I being punished because I have drowned my dog Tommy?"

"No, you already have been punished for that," said the Voice. "And we know why you killed your dog Tommy . . . because he bit your sister. You thought you were doing right, but you knew that you did wrong and you went out looking for days and days for your dog Tommy. You have learned that it is wrong to kill, and you have learned that if you do good things, you will get good things back, and if you do bad things, you will get bad things back. You have suffered for this wrong, and when you go back you will study the word of God and you will learn that there is also forgiveness. . . . But you will never kill anything again and you must use your gift for good so that others will not kill again. . . ."

Now Peter could feel a strange force running through his body. He could see the faces of the bearded figures all shrouded by a fog of light that seemed to roll down from the Big Master's chair, but he noticed that the beams of light in their eyes had turned on again and were piercing his body with heat.

He did not understand it but he knew there was something wrong with his body. It was that feeling of being two people again, as though part of him had stepped outside of himself and was standing beside him. He was more frightened than ever. He knew that his time in that other world was running out.

He asked again, "Why am I being punished if it is not for my dog Tommy?"

The Voice said, "You do not believe in the word of God. But this is not your fault. Your parents did not teach you to believe, but we will help you. When you go back and study the Bible, you will learn that the soul must be clean to enter the Lord's kingdom. You will learn that your gift is not from the devil but from the noble and clean souls you have met here. You have not finished your work in the world you come from, but when you go back you will work with the gift you take from here.

"Your gift will be a burden, a punishment, but you will learn to live with it and you must learn to believe in it, even when everyone else is against you. Many people you met here have had great gifts but they had to believe in them strongly when all the people were against them, and they believed strongly in the word of God." (Except Rasputin, apparently, but he was not one of the jurymen.)

Peter said, "I have not much education and I do not understand about the gift. Who will teach me to use the gift?"

The Voice said, "We will guide you. Your gift will come by inspiration, you cannot command it and it will not come at your bidding. But when it comes to you by inspiration, you must listen with your inner ear, and you will be able to contact the abstract world. You will remember what you saw here and you will hear the voice that will guide you."

"No, no!" Peter cried. "The Voice I hear in this world is good, kind. But please don't let me hear voices if you send me back. I'm afraid, so frightened now. . . . Please let me stay. . . ."

The Voice said, "Do not be afraid, Peter. Listen to the solitude within yourself, and when you hear our voice, remember that we are beside you, trying to help you. But you must not ask us questions when you hear the voice, you must not interrupt or we cannot stay with you. You must listen, only listen . . . and do what we tell you. . . . When you hear the voice, you will know that I am there with you. . . . I must leave now. . . . It is time for you to go back now, Peter, and start your new work. This is the completion of your journey here on a higher plane, a more noble plane than you came from. It is the end of a cycle in which you have learned much that you will use to help your people. . . . But we will see you again here someday when your time is ready. . . ."

Peter had listened, terrified at the thought of returning to a world filled with war and misery. He was beginning to remember it all now from that life before his fall.

Trembling and grasping at one last hope, he implored the jurymen, "Please, sirs, may I speak to the Master alone?"

"The Master has gone," the Voice said . . . and the Voice still came from the empty chair. At no time during the entire judgment solemnities was Peter able to detect even a shadowy substance of anyone occupying the chair. . . . Now the triangular light above it was beginning to dim. The bearded figures rose and said, "Come."

Peter noticed that the great round hall was empty of all the thousands of people he thought were there, but he had not heard them leave.

He followed the nine jurymen outside. He wanted desperately to talk to them again but when he tried, the words would not come. Now the nine men seemed to be more like a transfusion of celestial bodies, sometimes all in one iridescent chain of floating formlessness, sometimes separating in trailing clouds that billowed up and carried them off and then brought them back again. Indistinctly they faded and flickered in and out, in and out, in much the same way that images flicker and fade in and out on a television set that needs adjusting.

Peter followed them, running, stumbling, crying out to them, trying to reach them . . . until they were gone . . . in nine fast shooting streaks of light, like stars falling in the night.

He was alone now, and there before him was the opening in the mountains with the pyramid of light waiting for him. They had brought him this far. He looked around and behind him. . . . There was nothing . . . none of the happy little people and their *cupoles*, none of the beautiful clouds and colors and singing choirs . . . no half shells he could hide on as a stowaway to fly away and try to find that other world again.

He heard a voice say, "Good-by, Peter. Don't be afraid."

He walked to the mountains and into the light, and then he felt himself falling again . . . falling, falling, falling. His last thought as he left the other world was, Please don't let me go back to the darkness.

{16}

I Come Back

His guides in the other world kept their promise to Peter. He did not have to go back to the darkness.

"The falling from the other world was not the same as the first time," Peter remembered. "I went fast but I did not pass the darkness. It was like when you sleep and you fall into a deep pit, but then you wake up and it is not the blackness.

"But I was like a wild man, yelling and grabbing when I wake up and they had to tie me in the bed because I thought I was falling from the ladder again.

"I saw people moving and I heard voices but they were all far away, not real. . . . And there were not the beautiful colors here. Everything looked the same, gray and dirty. I was having trouble breathing the heavy air. I thought I was suffocating. I could feel that I was tied up in the bed and I was trying to get out. I was screaming, 'I want to go back there. I don't want to live. I want to die.'"

This is the way Peter remembers it. Many patients coming out of a deep coma think they're talking and are trying desperately to say something but cannot.

The doctors and nurses tried to calm him.

He was told later that once, when his mother and sister were standing at his bedside, he asked, "Who are you?"

His mother said, "Don't you remember me, Peter? I am your mother . . . and this is your sister, Allie."

"I never saw you before," he said. They turned away weeping.

His wife, Bea, stepped to his bedside and touched his forehead.

"Who are you? Why don't you leave me alone and let me go back. . . ."

It was days before Peter recognized his own family, but even then they realized there was a strangeness about him, a remoteness which in time would make him a complete stranger and cause them to shake their heads sadly and say, "This is not our Peter. He died and has come back in the same body, but there is someone else inside."

A great sadness comes over Peter when he talks about it. "When I came back, I did not have the same love for my family or my wife and child any more. I could not help it. My mind was not here."

In the hospital he had no appetite for food. He couldn't sleep. He suffered with severe headaches. "There was a terrible pressure in my head, like a rope was tied around my neck and I was about to explode. And sometimes when I did sleep, my mind was always awake but it was another mind, not my own. Somebody else inside of me."

His eyes couldn't focus. Everything was drab, colorless, and blurred—until the day that nurse Zelda put her palm on his forehead and he seemed to speak rationally for the first time. "Where am I?"

As nearly as we could reconstruct it from Peter's recollection, and from his family and members of the Zuidwal Hospital staff whom we were able to contact, nurse Zelda was the first person he recognized on his return to reality. That is, he at least recognized her as a nurse in a white uniform rather than a blurred image. She was present when he emerged briefly from that twilight sleep between consciousness and unconsciousness, and she was with him much of the time in the weeks that followed, for she was head nurse on his floor at the Zuidwal.

The hospital officials had told Stephy that nurse Zelda could tell us more about Peter than anyone else.

And I was even more certain of this after having met the Indonesian nurse, Ana Kaneel.

Ana had said that she was an assistant head nurse on Peter's floor. Then she must have known nurse Zelda. And she must have known what Peter told her that had terrified her so.

Nurse Zelda was the first person to experience the strange psychic world of Peter Hurkos. She was an unwitting midwife to his rebirth. She must have glimpsed that somebody else inside of him.

"Peter, do you remember nurse Zelda?" I asked.

"No. I had many nurses. I do not remember names."

"But do you remember the first one you recognized as a nurse when you woke up in the hospital?"

"Yes, sure. She was wearing a white uniform and I knew she was a nurse. So then I knew I was back in this world but I did not know where. Then she put her hand on my head and something happened to me." He paused.

"Can you tell us what happened, Peter?"

"My head was full of noises. I grabbed her hand and said, 'You better be careful when you go on the train, or else you lose your valise.' She looked at me strange and said, 'How did you know?' She told me she lost her suitcase that morning on the train already. I was frightened when she asked me how did I know. Then I remembered, this must be my gift. It was the first time. I didn't like it. How did I know what I didn't want to know?"

"Is that all you told her?"

"Yes. Why? After that I tell many things. . . ."

"Do you remember whether she was an Indonesian nurse?"

"No, we had many Indonesian nurses in the hospital."

"Do you remember some of the other things you told the nurses?"

"Oh, sure. Many things. Sometimes very bad things, too, and they hurt people. I didn't want to hurt anyone but I couldn't help it. I could not control my gift yet. I didn't know how to use it."

One day a nurse was washing his hands and face when he suddenly clasped her arm and said, "You are a nice person but it is a shame that you did not take care of your mother all the time she was living. You didn't take care of your own mother, and she was crippled."

The nurse drew back from him, shocked and frightened.

"How did you know that?" she stammered.

"Your mother was crippled for a long time," Peter said accusingly.

The nurse replied, "My mother was born crippled." She backed away, giving her patient a strange look, then ran from the room.

How did Peter know this?

"I saw a mental picture while she was washing me," he said. "A mental picture like on a TV screen. Her mother was sitting in a chair, and sometimes she didn't get her food on time, and the nurse didn't wash her mother like she did me. . . . Later I got very frightened because I knew about her mother. I said, What the hell am I talking about? How could I know this and I shouldn't say these things to people because it frightens them. But I was so frightened also because I didn't want to know these things. I knew there must be something wrong with my head."

He told a patient in the same room with him, "You are a bad man. . . . Your father died recently and left you a gold watch and you have sold it already." It was true.

He told one of the hospital staff that there was "false bookkeeping in the records and a big shortage of money." A supervisor came to his room and questioned him. An investigation proved he was correct.

The doctors finally told Peter he could get out of bed and start walking around the corridors to help get his strength back. They probably also wanted to know what would happen when he came in contact with other patients. By now word had spread throughout the hospital about the man with the third eye. Many had reported his strange "visions" to the doctors, who were skeptical at first, but as more and more reports came in from nurses, patients, and, yes, even some doctors (he told one about his illegitimate child from an affair with one of the nurses), the patient Pieter Cornelis van der Hurk became an object of great curiosity.

He wandered into one room and told a lung-patient, "You have a very serious problem with your lungs. But you don't have to be afraid to die. It is beautiful there . . . much better than here."

The frightened lung patient told the nurse, who reported it to the doctor. The patient died the next day. Although he was a terminal case, death had not been expected so soon. And how did Peter even know about the patient's lung problem?

A patient's wife was visiting him, sitting on his bed, when Peter walked in and said, "You have such a good husband, what a shame you are running around with other men. Why don't you quit?"

The woman glared at him and said nothing. Later he was to learn that this broke up their marriage, although it could not have been the only factor. The marriage must have been already floundering if the couple could take seriously the word of a man with the third eye.

Afterward, Peter knew that he shouldn't have said it, and he felt a great sense of guilt. "But it just came. Spontaneous. Like the valise and the crippled woman and the others. . . . I was like two different people. I have one mind in my head and another that comes out and takes control. One mind is more dominant . . . takes over the other. . . . I said, What is wrong with me? Why does my normal mind stay inside my body and my other mind comes out and sees these pictures? Then I say things I do not know about."

When you saw these things in the hospital, Peter, did you also hear a voice—or was it only the pictures?

"Oh, yes, yes, I hear the Voice. But I tell nobody that. I tell them only about the pictures. I could not tell them about the Voice or they think I'm crazy, mental case. They lock me up."

This is very important, Peter. We know that the Voice you al-

ways talk about now was that Voice *you heard in the other world.
But was this the same voice you heard in the hospital so soon
after you came back? Did you recognize it at once or were there
different voices?*

"At first it was sometimes different, like voices [Note the plu-
ral] in a language I could not understand. Then I recognized the
Voice from up there and it made me feel good to hear it again.
But sometimes I was mixed up when it was not the same voice.
And then panic started when the people ask, 'How does he
know?' 'How do you know?' They're right. How do I know?"

He has one terrible lingering memory of someone coming into
his room from time to time and trying to kill him, suffocate him
by holding a pillow over his head.

"I don't know who. I don't know why. Maybe some agent from
the underground. Maybe someone I frightened with what I told
them . . . maybe a nurse . . . I don't know . . . I don't
know. . . . But they are trying to suffocate me and I am gasping
for my breath."

Once, Peter recalls vividly, he looked at his hands and they
brought back all the far-remembered things from that other
world.

"I heard the music again and I saw all the people, so kind to me.
But then I look at my hands and they were not the soft skin that
I had before. They are rougher now. These are not my hands, I
say. Then I am frightened with myself. I ask, What am I doing
here? I do not belong here. . . ."

A doctor came in and said to Peter, "I hear you're supposed to
have the *helderziel* . . . the third eye."

"I didn't know what the third eye was then. I said, 'How could
I have a third eye? I have only two.' The doctor said he talked to
people around the hospital who say I see things like the third eye.
He said I should not talk to the people any more because it upsets
them. He told me it's God's gift that I can see deeper than most
people, and I have to live with it. But I should not upset the
other people in the hospital."

I asked Peter once more about nurse Zelda. Yes, the name was
familiar to him, he said, but only because he had heard so much

about her. People had told him that she was his head nurse and the one he warned about losing her valise. But there were too many nurses and doctors and other people moving in and out of his life during those weeks of July and August 1941 when he was trying to re-enter the world of reality. His memories are blurred not only by the years of interminable self-torment but by the "somebody else" who had possession of his body at that time.

It is understandable how he would have no clear memory of nurse Zelda.

Still, I asked, "Can you remember telling her, or any of the nurses, to be careful because there was going to be a big fire, an explosion?"

He thought about it a long time. "No. No," he said quietly. "I know I told many bad things and I am sorry. But I don't remember that. Could be it was when somebody else took over my mind. But it would not be the man with the beard—up there."

Four days after Peter was discharged from the hospital, on August 5, 1941, he bought a secondhand Bible in the market for two guilders and began reading it from cover to cover. He even slept with his Bible. He found he could sleep better with it, even in the darkness.

"I bought the Bible because the people up there in the other world told me I was not religious and I must learn about God. So I took my Bible into the mountains and studied it, and I got a little more understanding," Peter said. "But my mother and father and sister all laughed at me. Even my father said, 'Pieter is different. Why don't you throw that damn thing away. You eat with the Bible, you go to sleep with the Bible, always the Bible!' . . . We never had a Bible in the house before, and they were all laughing at me. But I read it back and forth, chapter by chapter. . . . It was printed in Dutch. . . . And I learned many things from it. I learned there is forgiveness when you have done wrong and I got peace from this for what I did to my dog Tommy. . . . I was learning how to control my gift and not hurting people. . . . So one mind was going straight and the other mind—I tried not to think about it. . . . I study my Bible and sometimes 1 get peace of mind. . . ."

But in the world of reality, Peter continued to be bewildered by the gift he could not comprehend. He became more and more alienated from his wife and his family. He would take his Bible and go out to the mountains or the sea and sit alone.

He became a recluse, although he discovered the wonder of small children.

"Sometimes when I was studying the Bible, the little children would come up to me, and I would play with them and tell them stories. I felt more comfortable with children because they had a clean mind, they were not bad like people. They were honest and they would listen to me. They never asked me, 'How do you know?' like other people and they didn't laugh at me. When I was with them, my gift went away and I would have a normal mind. And when I was with them I even felt like a child. I had peace of mind.

"But sometimes I would go to the mountains and try to find that same place where I had been in the other world and I couldn't. Then I would be unhappy again. . . ."

Peter was still receiving outpatient medical care. Doctors were mystified by his "hallucinatory" symptoms, which, unlike those of most psychotic or brain-damaged patients, so frequently revealed his third eye (the most common Dutch term for a sixth sense or psychic ability) that could perceive things beyond the normal sensory faculties. But Peter thought it was a sign of insanity.

He kept asking himself, Was this the great gift those people up there had promised him?

He would ask the doctors, "Why can't you make these things go away?"

And all they could say was, "There are many things about the mind we do not know and cannot explain. The *helderziel* is one of them. [*Helderziel* is the Dutch word for psychic or clairvoyant] It is God's gift and you must learn to live with it."

They often tried to reassure him by the reminder: "You have

had a very severe head injury, and you are an extremely lucky man to be alive."

But most of the time Peter did not feel at all lucky to be alive. His headaches continued. The pressure was often unbearable. At times his head felt as though it was splitting open, not only with pain but with the sounds and the visions from his third eye. He was trying very hard to believe it was God's gift. The Voice up there had told him he must learn to believe.

"I was trying to understand while I was studying the Bible, and I really wanted to believe," he said. "I thought if I learned to believe strong enough, like the Voice said, the gift that was my punishment would go away."

But it didn't. People soon were lined up outside his mother's house for private "readings" from the *helderziende,* for one guilder each.

Peter and his wife, Bea, had separated. His strange gift had become as intolerable to her as it was to him, and so he moved in with his parents. It was his mother's idea to put his gift to use, partly to keep him occupied but also because they needed the money. Before his fall, and during the Nazi occupation of Holland, Peter had been a member of the Dutch underground. Working at any job now was not easy for him because he had lost his ability to concentrate for any period of time. But occasionally his gift came in handy for "reading" maps for the underground and reporting his psychic interpretations.

When the war was over his mother pushed him into giving public performances to demonstrate his gift. He was billed as Helder Ziende, the great clairvoyant, or "The Man With the Gift." (Clairvoyant or psychic: *helder*—clear; *ziende*—seeing.) He became a great success but he didn't like it. He left Holland and went to France, where he began working with the police on criminal cases—just as the seer had prophesied he would. Some of the cases were reported in newspapers, and his fame spread. He was soon in demand throughout Europe, where he also became known as the man with the "radar eyes" and the "X-ray brain."

"I became more interested in working with police on crime cases, especially murders, because I hated people who killed little children or other people, and I wanted to help stop the murderers," Peter explained. "Also it made me feel better that I was using my gift for good, like the Voice up there told me, and I think that is why the Voice guides me so much in my police cases."

The Voice had also told him his gift would go in many directions, and amazingly it led him to a position as psychic consultant to a medical doctor in Paris who was working on a new polio serum. Peter had no previous training or background in medicine, of course, but his work as a psychic consultant and medical researcher was so astounding that it was reported in *Paris Match* magazine. It was this report that brought him to the attention of American parapsychologists, who sponsored his entry to this country in 1956 for ESP tests and observation.

Meanwhile, however, another one of Peter's psychic gifts—and one of the most baffling—had emerged only about a month after he was discharged from the hospital. This was his gift for music. His mother had taken him to visit a friend who was a professional concert pianist and teacher. So far as Peter can remember he had rarely ever seen a piano before, maybe in school or in a theater, and he had never tried nor even wanted to play one. But as he was walking past the woman's piano, he suddenly stopped and said, "Do you know your piano needs tuning?"

Then he sat down and began moving his hands over the keyboard, first slowly and as though listening to something far away. And presently he was playing strange music with fingers that seemed to know where they were going, as sure as though they had been playing all his life.

"I didn't know Peter could play the piano," the woman said to Peter's mother.

"I didn't know it either," Peter's mother replied. She was as startled as her pianist friend.

"Where did he learn to play the piano?" the friend asked.

Peter's mother could only shake her head and say, "I don't

know. I don't understand it. I have never seen him ever touch a piano."

Peter stopped playing, looked up at them, and said, "I have never played the piano before."

The pianist-teacher looked at him oddly, and then at his mother, with arched eyebrows that plainly meant she didn't believe it. She didn't recognize any of the music, she said. "It's beautiful, but it sounds strange. Where did you learn to play that kind of music?" she asked Peter. "I don't know," he said. Why should he tell them? He knew they would laugh at him.

Something had continued to puzzle me from the time I met Ana Kaneel. Now that I knew when Peter's gift for music was discovered, so soon after his fall, I was puzzled all the more. All of his psychic gifts except one—painting—were discovered, or developed, while he was still in the Zuidwal Hospital or soon after he was discharged.

Why was his gift for painting so long in emerging? Or was it?

Peter insisted that he had never painted in Holland. Yet Ana Kaneel knew him as a painter and even had one of his paintings which he had given her while he was in Zuidwal, she said.

I knew that we had to meet with Ana Kaneel soon. Stephy and I both were anxious to ask her about nurse Zelda. In fact, Stephy was still hoping that Ana might turn out to be nurse Zelda. Tess, who had worked with Peter long enough to take a more realistic view of things, was sure we would be wasting our time in meeting with nurse Ana.

"She's probably just another fan who's read about Peter and wants to meet him. I'll bet she never saw the inside of the Zuidwal and isn't even a nurse. You'd be surprised at some of the weirdos Peter attracts," Tess said.

Nevertheless, I intended to see Ana Kaneel and have a look at the painting Peter gave her.

"She's crazy lady," he grumbled. "I did not do paintings in

Holland. Only here. Anyway, you get me too deep in with the paintings."

"Okay, forget it," I said.

It was important to tread gently with Peter. He couldn't be pushed into anything until he was ready.

{17}

Don't Be Afraid to Die

Oh, Flammarion, have pity on me. . . . You, an astronomer
and a thinker . . . I beg you on my knees, tell me if our souls survive somewhere. . . . Say something to me, you who possess the secrets of the heavens! You who know! We simple mortals can neither
know or understand. Tell me if the souls survive somewhere, if they
remember, if they still love those who remain on earth; if they see
us, if we can call them near us. . . .

FLAMMARION
Death and Its Mystery

Excerpt from a letter—"To Our Great Flammarion" . . .
from N. Bofford, Reinosa, Spain,
March 30, 1907

. . . a widow who wants to communicate
with her dead son

No one knows what death is, and whether it be not the greatest of all good things for Man. Nevertheless, it is feared as though it were the supreme evil. . . .

When death comes near to Man, that which is mortal in him is scattered, that which is immortal and incorruptible withdraws intact.

SOCRATES

LET ME SAY AT THE START THAT IT IS NOT MY PURPOSE HERE TO postulate any theories about the so-called hereafter.

I remain in that middle road between believing and disbelieving, with the open road ahead of me, and an open mind like a filtering sieve leaning a little toward skepticism.

But this is Peter's story, not mine.

The supreme question of whether we are ephemeral or lasting, of whether or not we survive death, has remained so far outside the sphere of the recognized sciences—and certainly out of mine. As the philosopher Flammarion said, "The dweller upon this earth is a strange being. He lives upon a planet without knowing where he is and without having the curiosity to ask himself—without seeking to know his nature . . . !

"Something survives the disintegration of the earthly body . . . that 'something' can be called a principle, an element, a psychic atom, a soul, or a spirit. . . . It matters little. . . . The body dies, the soul lives on in the infinite and the eternal. . . ."

This was precisely what Peter had been saying, though he had never heard of Flammarion, much less read about him.

The questions had to be put to Peter in simple terms.

When you were up there with all those souls, Peter, could you communicate, could you talk with the people down here?

"No. I did not remember anybody down here, not my mother or my father or my dog."

You had no remembrance, no feeling for anyone in this world?

"No. None. But you see, dear, I was not really dead yet. I was only there by mistake."

Yes, but you were with all the other souls. Did they ever communicate—talk to the people down here?

"No. Never. Oh, yes, they talk. But the people here cannot talk back. It is like the Voice told me, I hear it, I listen to what it say to me but I do not ask questions."

Do they remember their life from this world, their families, their work, the things that happened to them?

"Sure they remember. What do you mean they remember? One of the men with the beard tell me how much the Church is against him but still he believes, very strong."

Do you remember who this man was, Peter? You didn't mention him before.

"No. All the same. I can't tell you everything I saw, all together. He was one of the jurymen, very intellectual, like a scientist or something, always looking at stars. . . ."

Could you see stars up there, Peter?

"Oh, yes, sure, stars brighter than here, and I saw other planets too, far away. But I did not see this planet here."

Now, stop and think a minute, Peter. We were talking about communication between the souls up there and the people—their families and loved ones they left down here. People down here want to know—is there any way they can communicate with those who have died?

"I tell you only what I know from up there. They are very happy in that other world. They do not think too much about this world. But they remember. . . . And they are sad only when they remember. . . .

"You cannot talk to them but you can listen to the Voice when it comes. And you can see the pictures when they come.

"But I tell you something. You must be developed on a higher plane than this to be in contact with them."

What do you mean by that? How do you get on a higher plane to contact the souls?

"I mean the people here have not much understanding. You have to believe what you can do. That's what they told me there, that I must believe. I never saw Jesus or God or whatever it is. I only saw the empty chair. But I studied the Bible and now I believe strongly in the Lord. I don't believe in any church. I believe in the mountains if I want to pray. If I am emotionally upset, if you are emotionally upset, just go there, sit there by yourself and pray what comes to you, and then you get the answer.

"You do not get the answer in the church. There are many churches but God's house is an open house for rich or poor, and you cannot buy a chair in it like in the church. That is not in the Bible. . . . In God's house you are not allowed to marry or die first class, or second class or third class. The house is built in God's name and the people use it wrong. . . . You have to go in to the mountains and pray deeply and meditate and rest the mind. The mind is too much on troubles to hear the Voice from up there."

Do you mean that only those of us down here who are able to progress to a higher plane can make contact with the souls in the other world?

"Yes. Definitely."

What do you mean by a higher plane?

"I mean you must be higher developed in your mind if you want to reach them, contact them. They are much higher developed in the mind than we are. They can talk to you but you can't hear them because your mind is not developed so strong in that direction.

"My mind is developed—not by education, but by what I saw in the other world, what they show me and tell me and teach me. So I hear the Voice and I see the pictures when they come. But they do not always make me happy. I tell you I would be the happiest man in the world if I could switch them off. What I remember from the other world is too beautiful to remember, and makes me want to go back. So maybe it is better if you don't contact the souls there. Makes you feel worse they're so happy. . . ."

When you speak of being "higher developed" in the mind, do you mean only intellectually—or something else?

"Intellectual, yes. I mean all the people up there, the men with the beards were very highly intellectual. But down here I mean the mind can be developed other ways.

"The mind is the whole body, the strongest part of your body. The mind can control the body. The mind can save the body. I give you example—my own operation. When I was out of my body and watched my hip operation. At first I didn't think I would come out of it, and I was frightened. Then the Voice came and told me to get the flowers for my room, to have oxygen and energy, and the Voice told me I would be walking in fourteen days.

"But my mind has to believe what the Voice is telling me. I have to build up in my mind, I am going to walk, I am going to be okay, I am not going to die. I have different feelings about this. Sometimes I think I want to go back to that other world where it was so beautiful, but then I know I have to stay here with Stephy. So my mind listens to the Voice and he tells me I'm going to be okay, I'm going to walk, no infection, no nothing. . . .

"And I build that up in my mind, I do just what the Voice tells me. . . . I build up energy with the flowers, I build up the courage with my mind, I concentrate strongly and I get well so fast even the doctors didn't believe it. But I did it with my mind. The mind can heal the body, the mind can save the body, the mind can do anything it wants to do. . . ."

You said at first you were frightened, Peter, when you thought you might not come out of your operation. Did you have a fear of dying?

"Oh, no, no, no. How could I be afraid of dying again when it was so beautiful and I feel so good when I am there. Not the fall, no, or the darkness, but this time it wouldn't be the fall or the darkness. Only the operation. And everybody is frightened of operations. Also I was thinking of Stephy. But one thing I can say to the people for sure, don't be afraid to die. Death feels good when you are there. I would never be afraid to die again. Never."*

* Dr. Elisabeth Kuebler-Ross, a Swiss-born doctor on the staff of Cook County Hospital in Chicago, recently reported (Los Angeles *Times*, March 9, 1975) on the reactions of several hundred patients who had been declared medically dead and had come back. "Those who have been there—or close— say it feels good. Death is a feeling of peace and wholeness. . . . The patients can describe in minute detail what they experience and how they float out of their body. . . . The most common denominator of all these people is that when they come back, many of them resented our desperate attempts to bring them back. Not one of them has ever been afraid to die again."

{18}

Who Am I?

I have been here before,
But when or how I cannot tell. . . .
                    D. G. ROSSETTI
                    Sudden Light

THE QUESTION OF REINCARNATION WAS INEVITABLE, AND I WAS totally unprepared for Peter's reaction to it.

I am neither a believer nor disbeliever in reincarnation. My mind is still open.

Modern science, of course, completely discredits the concept of a previous existence and the rebirth of a soul in another body. Nevertheless, millions of people the world over believe in it.

The doctrine of reincarnation has had a long and fascinating history, originating probably with the ancient sages of India. Among the Greeks it was taught by Pythagoras and Plato and has been accepted by many thoughtful men, notably poets and philosophers. One common belief is that some form of pre-existence may explain child geniuses, such as Mozart or Chopin, as well as mathematical prodigies and others with outstanding gifts or talents that cannot be otherwise explained.

The theme of reincarnation has become one of the most popular and best-selling story plots in today's movie, television, and book markets. But in trying to reconstruct "The Reincarnation of Peter Hurkos" we were led into a labyrinth of perplexities.

There was no question that Peter was better qualified for reincarnation than most people who proclaim themselves to have been somebody else in a previous life.

His four days of unconsciousness is medically documented. Science acknowledges the out-of-body phenomenon as an actuality. There is no way scientifically to prove or disprove Peter's account of where he was or what happened to him. But there is no reason to question the sincerity of his belief.

He had seen the souls of some of the great men of history. When he stood before the jury in the other world he had experienced for the first time that feeling of a double being, a double consciousness or double mind, that he was to bring back with him to this world. He had felt a strange force entering his body, the power from the beams of light in the eyes of the nine men on the jury.

There was no question that he had experienced some form of rebirth when he returned to this earth, that he had been reborn, as his parents said, with somebody else in his body.

If there is any one single truth Peter knows about himself beyond all others, it is this: that he is not the same Pieter Cornelis van der Hurk who existed before his fall. He is somebody else and the transformation took place during his out-of-body experience in the other world.

This truth torments him and stays with him every day of his life. It does not go away. Nor does he derive any pride, pleasure, or comfort in being told the probable or possible identities of his guides in the other world.

Most of the names we tried to match with his descriptions meant little or nothing to him.

"But who am I? Who is me?" he would ask over and over.

Even the composer, with whom he seemed to feel the closest identity, could not provide the missing link to Peter's other self.

Anyone else would have leaped at the chance to be a reincarnated Beethoven—or da Vinci or Galileo or Nostradamus. But not Peter.

Always when I read the biographical notes to him or tried to explain certain similarities between the other-world images he saw and their once-living counterparts here, he would listen attentively and sometimes express mild curiosity with one word: "Ya?" The comparisons clearly didn't penetrate.

He always returned to that same question, "But who am I?"

That other great psychic, Edgar Cayce, apparently had no problem convincing himself (and millions of others) that he was the great Priest Ra-Ta (son of the Sun God, Ra) in his previous incarnation in Egypt. Why couldn't Peter have had a previous incarnation as at least *one* of those nine jurymen he met in the other world?

It would have made a great ending for our book. He was not about to oblige us by fulfilling such fantasies.

Of all the incredible facets of this man, Peter Hurkos, none to me was more astonishing than his complete and absolute rejection of reincarnation as an answer to who he is.

But at least it saved us the bother of scouting through graveyards all over the world trying to track down his incarnated ancestry.

At a time when the concept of reincarnation was reaching a mystical high pitch, when more and more people were proclaiming to be somebody else in a previous life, Peter remained one of those curiously perplexing oddities who disclaimed knowledge of any pre-existence whatsoever—except that of Pieter Cornelis van der Hurk.

He bristled at the slightest suggestion that he was a "reincarnated" Beethoven, Nostradamus, or anyone else.

"Do you understand what reincarnation is?" I asked him.

"Oh, sure. I was reborn into somebody else," he said.

"Have you ever felt that you were somebody else in another existence?"

"No. Never."

"When you saw the composer up there, and the painter, and the others, did you feel that you had lived their lives before?"

"No. What I got there was inspiration, not reincarnation," he insisted.

"But you mentioned that sometimes you go far back in time."

"Yes. Definite. I go back many times. But it is only the feeling I get from the people. I did not live anybody's life."

"You have never had the feeling that you were somebody else in another life?"

"Somebody else in this life, yes. I was Pieter van der Hurk. But no other life. One is enough. Are you kidding?"

"But all of those men you saw up there—don't you think it's possible that you might have been one of them before, in another life?"

"No. How could I be when I was living my own life . . . Peter the Fisherman. I was only a sailor and a house painter."

I was deliberately testing him. "Now, Peter, think carefully about those nine men you saw up there. Try to remember each one individually, if you can. If you could come back in another life sometime, which of those men would you like to be? Who would you rather be than Peter Hurkos?"

He didn't even have to think about it. He looked at me and said, without hesitating, "A sailor. Yes, if I could come back in another life, I would rather be a sailor. . . . Or a fisherman. . . . That is the only time when I find peace of mind."

If Peter had not lived previous lives as any of the nine men who gave him his gift, how did he get it and what did he mean by saying he had other lives?

"Remember, Peter, you said that you have had many lives. Otherwise how would you know how to play music or paint or have your psychic gift? And you said that everyone has had other lives, too," I reminded him.

"Yes. But I do not mean they have lived the life of that person. I mean we are all part of many lives," he explained. "All of those who have passed before us and those who come are part of us but in a different time as we know it. In the other world, in the psychic world, time has no meaning. From the beginning to the end is now. Nothing is impossible in the psychic world. Today this is all strange. In a hundred years or more it will be normal. For me it was the wrong time, a mistake. But I was there, so I saw what it is like.

"We go to different planes, different levels. I know it from up there. I was on a higher plane there and they gave me part of it to bring back with me. It is like an abstract world . . . no time, no space. You can only contact the abstract world when you learn to be alone, in solitude. There is no devil in the abstract world. Only good people, clean people, some who have to come back many times when the soul is clean and pure. That is what I know about reincarnation. You go from many planes and you learn from inspiration, not reincarnation. Nobody lives the life of anybody else but they are all up there in that other world. . . . And they give me their gift. That's what I mean when I say I have many lives."

Somehow this made more sense to me than if he had said he was Prince Ra-Ta in a previous incarnation.

Without knowing it, Peter was expressing beliefs closely akin to the teachings of yoga and the biological-spiritual progression on different planes to a higher consciousness.

Peter knows nothing about the teachings of yoga or the philosophy of the Indian mystics. He apparently didn't even have a nodding acquaintance with any of them in the other world, although it is in the cults and culture of India that reincarnation has its firmest foothold.

I have always believed that Peter's psychic faculties have a biological basis. Genetic memory, for example, may one day be proved a scientific fact. It is already widely accepted in India by scientists and philosophers exploring the familiar phenomenon of déjà vu (the feeling of having been there before) as well as the concept of reincarnation. If a child can inherit physical features from his parents, why can't he inherit memory "engravings" from a long-distant past? Scientists are still exploring the complex memory mechanisms of the human brain. When they find out how memory operates—how we remember and forget—they will have unlocked one of the most fascinating mysteries of the mind.

There is also the theory that individual memory is indestructible, that the memory of an individual is written in indelible script in space and time, and becomes an eternal part of a cosmos in development.

Is it possible that Peter acquired some of the "indestructible" memory of those nine men he met in the other world?

Did he bring back flashes of genius and perception from some of the great men of history—or is he simply a psychopath? There is sometimes a fine line between genius and insanity, just as some psychic manifestations sometimes border on the psychotic.

What was happening within Peter's physiological brain-mind mechanisms during those four days he lay unconscious in the Zuidwal?

Where did all his visionary experiences come from? The colors, the music, the bearded guides and their gifts? Did they come from other worlds? From previous lives? Of whom? And how? They came from somewhere, and one thing seems fairly certain: they did somehow originate within the biological chemistry of his own brain. He did not manufacture them out of his imagination. He is not that imaginative. They had nothing to do with religious, mystical, or supernatural beliefs. At the time he was devoid of such beliefs.

There are many nonmystical subconscious channels into the past, and the future: electrical brain stimulation, the mind-expanding drugs, hypnosis, meditation, psychic trances, sleep, and dreams. Cold, hard scientific research has established that under certain conditions the human brain does indeed manifest various "supernormal," "abnormal," or "superhuman" phenomena that so far have not been explained.

Peter's subconscious channels into a "universal consciousness," as Edgar Cayce called it, were produced by a brain injury. His venture into reincarnation, if it was that, was the physical, *not* metaphysical, transformation that resulted from landing on his head on a concrete pavement when he fell from a four-story house painter's ladder.

It is even possible that Peter experienced a form of what Russian scientists call "artificial reincarnation." After visiting both Russia and India on previous parapsychological research trips, I am convinced that scientists in both countries are far ahead of us in exploring the nature of man's brain-mind mechanisms. Soviet scientists, for example, have long used hypnosis as a tool for studying telepathy, clairvoyance, and other forms of psychic phenomena. They are now experimenting with "artificial reincarnation" through hypnosis, as a method of developing hidden talents.

Art students, for example, can be regressed in a hypnotic trance and made to think they are Raphael or da Vinci, and the Soviets claim this helps them to draw better and to learn to do so faster, and sometimes in a style similar to Raphael or da Vinci. One master hypnotist supposedly has "reincarnated" one of his students as a nineteenth-century artist, and is trying to evoke the birth of talent, perhaps even genius, in his other students.

Few people, if any, realize the extraordinary powers they possess, and according to the Soviet scientists, artificial reincarnation allows the mind to operate on new, almost "magical" laws. They feel it can be useful in artistic, musical, and scientific training.

Well, why not? Volumes have been written on the wonders performed by the mind under hypnosis. Is it too far-fetched to believe that if an art student is regressed and told he is Raphael, he might learn to paint faster and better?

Peter was in a state of coma, not hypnosis, during those four days after his fall. But is it too far-fetched to wonder whether those same—or similar—brain-mind mechanisms that take over in a hypnotic trance could become activated in a state of coma from a brain injury? I am only asking. It is for scientists studying the brain to come up with the answers. So far American brain-mind scientists have largely ignored hypnosis as a tool for the exploration of man's mind.

Is it possible that Peter's brain injury produced a kind of instant artificial reincarnation of the men he saw in his out-of-body world?

He makes no such claims. This is beyond his comprehension or imagination. But I am asking the question in the hope that one day scientists will regard such mental phenomena as at least worthy of serious investigation.

This would be a giant step up from their usual apathetic reminder of something we already know—that our knowledge of ourselves is fragmentary and incomplete.

While Soviet scientists are making new discoveries about the mind through hypnosis, medical doctors and scientists in India are engaged in neurophysiological research on the yogi's psychosomatic control of his body and breathing, which sometimes has the appearance of supernormal powers. I visited the All Indian Institute of Medical Sciences in New Delhi where the yogi research was in full progress (with some provocative conclusions which I reported in *The Psychic World of Peter Hurkos*) and talked with leading scientists and scholars throughout India. Almost all were in agreement over the fact that healthy forms of yoga and mental and spiritual disciplines can lead to the development of psychic faculties.

They also were in general agreement that the true yogi's seemingly supernormal powers of perception and mind control, which some people mistakenly refer to as *extra*sensory perception, is not *extra*sensory at all, but purely sensory—a highly refined extension and development of the normal sensory organs and powers that are latent in everyone, if we wish to develop them.

Gopi Krishna's word for this is *kundalini,* a concept that is gaining acceptance among an increasing number of scientists and interested laymen in many parts of the world.

Gopi Krishna is a scientist-philosopher from Srinagar (in Kashmir) who founded the Institute for Kundalini for research into the psychophysiological organism of man. Its purpose is to determine the nature of the biological processes responsible for the generation of the psychic force at the root of all transhuman states of consciousness and paranormal faculties.

Kundalini, according to Krishna, is a kind of brain-power mechanism responsible for man's evolution.

His theory is that all of us have a powerful reservoir of psychic energy, which, when roused to activity, can lead to transcendental states of consciousness, genius, and supernormal psychic gifts.

Research into *kundalini*, which Krishna calls the "evolutionary energy in man," has contributed further evidence that psychic talents originate *not* by some supernatural process but by a biological mechanism within the human brain.

In his book *Higher Consciousness* (Julian Press, 1974), he writes:

> There is no explanation for these sudden flashes of insight or sudden development of precocious talents, sometimes even without education, unless we admit the existence of a dormant faculty in the human brain that works more or less erratically and often independently of the deliberate thought of a person. . . . It is these extraordinary faculties—the essential attributes of a higher state of consciousness—that the ancient Indian treatises on Yoga and the occult have described as the *vibhutis,* or *siddhis,* or the opening of the "Third Eye." . . .
>
> . . . These psychic faculties form part of an evolutionary perfection toward which the whole race is inching its way, slowly but inexorably carried forward by certain biological changes occurring in the cerebral system of man.
>
> . . . It is important to know the law underlying the phenomena and the nature of the force responsible for them. . . . Whatever mankind has achieved till now it owes either to the man of genius and talent or to the prophet and seer. . . . There is a stupendous, fantastic universe which can only be approached through mind and consciousness, or, in other words perceived by an inner eye of the soul. . . . But during the last two centuries science has completely ignored and even blocked this vital channel of information. . . .
>
> . . . The appearance throughout history of enlightened prophets, mystics, geniuses, prodigies, and individuals possessing uncommon psychic faculties, is a clear testimony in support of the fact that there do exist hidden possibilities in the brain of man about which science has no knowledge at present.

Most of us would not wish to achieve this "higher consciousness" in the same way Peter did.

He came back to this world a man possessed by many lives within one body. They cannot be exorcised. When he asks, "Who am I?" there is no answer . . . only—"somebody else."

Does that somebody else have an identity, or is it a fusion of all those he met on his out-of-body plane of consciousness?

Of one thing I am certain: Peter's body is possessed by somebody else, by different entities at different times and different places. I had sensed this on many occasions—while he was working on cases, or psychometrizing articles and photographs (such as Beethoven's), or playing the organ or painting.

But I realized it for the first time with rather frightening certainty one evening when I glanced up at the baby, Gloria Ann, in her highchair and saw something I had been searching for a long time to find—the child's face Peter had subconsciously painted in his clouds of "Mur Woods."

No wonder the little boy's face in the clouds had looked familiar to me when I first saw it!

I had known Gloria Ann since she was born and had seen her often during all the months since Peter first showed us his "Mur Woods" painting. But not until now did I recognize her as the face in the clouds, the one Peter always called a little boy—the man with the beard as a child.

It was Peter's child, but he had painted the picture while Stephy was still pregnant. And he didn't even know he was painting faces in the clouds.

How could he have had foreknowledge of what his baby would look like at age two—before she was even born? What spirit entity had possession of his body while he was painting "Mur Woods"?

The thought was deeply disturbing. I said nothing about it yet to Peter and Stephy. But I asked to borrow "Mur Woods" for a while. I wanted to take it home and study it.

I also knew that the time had come when we had to see Ana Kaneel.

If she really had been his nurse at the Zuidwal and knew about his rebirth as a psychic and a painter, surely she could give us some clues to his other self or other mind that takes over and possesses his body.

{19}

The Forger

IT WAS EARLY EVENING WHEN WE DROVE UP A WINDING ROAD HIGH above Sunset Boulevard and found the steep driveway to Ana Kaneel's home. It was a rambling house, hidden far back from the road among a dark junglelike overgrowth of tropical foliage and wild orchids.

Ana Kaneel greeted us at the door wearing a hostess gown of oriental silk print. There was still an air of remoteness and mystery about her. Or was it only my imagination? Something she had said to me flashed through my mind: "I am an oriental psychic and perhaps we understand these things better than you."

For some curious reason I suddenly had an uneasy feeling that one psychic at a time was enough for me to cope with, that I had made a mistake in bringing the two of them together. I am not usually smitten by good or bad "vibes" but no one could have missed the strange vibrations between these two when they met.

Ana looked at Peter anxiously, as though trying to place the face, then said lightly, "So you are the great Peter Hurkos."

Peter was embarrassed. "Do I know you from Holland?" he asked awkwardly.

"Yes. Don't you remember? . . ." She began speaking to him in Dutch. Then to us: "Would you like to see the gardens? Come." She took Peter's arm and led the way while we trailed behind.

She continued speaking to him in Dutch. He replied in monosyllables, "Ya, ya."

I sensed that he was uncomfortable. Finally I suggested that we go inside to talk.

The house was California contemporary with a decor of modest elegance. The living room was dominated by a large stone fireplace and a grand piano. Ana wheeled in a teacart and served us Indonesian cakes and soft drinks around the fireplace.

Stephy opened the conversation by getting right to the point.

"Are you nurse Zelda?" she asked.

"No. My name is Ana." She appeared unruffled at the question.

"Did you know nurse Zelda? Do you know where she is?"

"Yes, I knew her, of course. I do not know where she is now. That was many years ago."

"You knew about Peter's accident? You were there at the Zuidwal after his fall?"

"Yes, of course."

"What do you remember about it—about the way Peter was when he came back?" Stephy asked eagerly.

"I remember it well," said Ana. "I remember how the nurses were frightened to go into his room because they never knew what he might tell them. He told me many things and all of them have come true . . . about the two letters in the pocket of my uniform, the death of my parents, and the man I was going to marry."

"Do you remember any of this?" I asked Peter.

"No. But I tell many things I do not remember," he replied moodily.

He was staring blankly into space. He appeared to be in a state of mental dissociation, without a glimmer of recognition of Ana Kaneel, or remembrance of anything she was talking about.

"He was in a comatose state. That's why he doesn't remember," Ana explained.

"He was in a coma," Stephy corrected.

"Yes, at first a coma. But then he would lapse in and out of consciousness. There are many comatose stages," Ana said. "Sometimes a patient can hear everything around him and he tries to talk but he cannot talk. Sometimes he really thinks he is talking when he is not talking. Sometimes he is talking, but incoherently."

I asked, "Did you ever hear Peter talk about a voice, or talking with a voice? Did you hear him talking to anyone else—like maybe someone who wasn't there?"

She was looking directly at me as I spoke. I noticed the slight tightening of her small shoulders and the momentary flash of terror in her eyes. "No," she said, rather abruptly. Behind her inscrutable mask I knew there was something else she had to tell me, but not here.

She quickly changed the subject.

"I just remembered, I have something I want to show Peter."

She left the room and returned with something clutched in her hand. She placed it in Peter's hand and closed his fingers over it. "Do you know what this is?" she asked.

"Yes, a coin." That would have been easy enough to know by touch. "I gave it to you . . . from the drawer by my bed," he said.

"Yes. Now you do remember?"

"Yes. Now I remember."

I asked Ana, "Do you still have that painting you said Peter gave to you while he was in the hospital?"

"Yes. It is a beautiful painting. I will always treasure it because Peter gave it to me. It is an exact replica of a painting in a museum in Holland by a very famous Dutch painter."

"Where is it? May we see it?"

"Of course. If I can find it. I have it put away."

She excused herself and went to look for it, but soon returned saying, "I can't find it right now. I'll get it for you later."

I thought it rather odd that she could not find Peter's painting, particularly since she knew that he was coming to her home.

"Do you remember painting a picture for her, Peter?" I asked.

"Oh, he wouldn't remember, he painted so many pictures," Ana said. "Remember how you were painting all over the walls and sheets and pillowcases, Peter?"

"Ya, ya," he nodded agreeably.

"How long did you know Peter in the hospital?" I asked.

"About two or three months, I think. . . ."

I knew this couldn't be right. Stephy blurted out, "But Peter wasn't in the hospital that long. Do you remember what year you had Peter as a patient?"

"I think it was 1948 or 1949. It was after the war."

We were all puzzled at this. "Oh, no, it was not after the war, it was during the war when Peter had his fall," Stephy said. We all knew the dates when Peter was in the hospital—from July 10 to August 5, 1941, we told her.

Even Peter spoke up then. "Yes, it was 1941. During the occupation. My father and I were painting buildings for the Germans."

"But I am speaking of Peter's second time in the hospital," Ana said.

We all reacted with astonishment. "What do you mean, his second time? Peter was never in the hospital a second time, were you, Peter?"

Peter was looking up strangely at Ana Kaneel. He didn't answer. In all the years we had known him, he had never once mentioned a word to any of us about being in the Zuidwal a second time. And up to now, Ana had talked as if she had known him as a patient immediately after his fall.

It was a curious turn of events and very perplexing.

"Why was he admitted the second time?" I asked. "What was wrong with him?"

"Pressure on the brain. He was having seizures, symptoms of epilepsy. They had to bore holes and drain the brain cavity to relieve the pressure. It was a new kind of operation then. It was done by two doctors from Spain," said Ana.

"Do you remember any of this, Peter?" we asked. "Do you remember being in the hospital a second time?"

"Ya, ya . . . pressure on the brain . . . like she said."

"Why haven't you ever said anything about this to us?"

"I didn't remember it until now."

"But now you do remember?"

"Sure . . ."

But how could we be sure? Was he just going along with Ana, or did he really remember? Was his response simply an expression of his deep yearning to have a normal brain that remembers what it was meant to remember? Or was he trying to forget something that Ana had told him?

I knew that either Ana or Peter, or both, were holding back something, but this was neither the time nor the place to pursue it. I would have to see her alone.

We said our good-bys and, as we walked toward the door, Ana said, "May I ask you to answer just one question for me, Peter?"

"What is that?"

"How long am I going to live?"

"I never tell people things like that. I'm tired now," he said. "We have to go."

In the car, easing down the steep driveway toward the lights of the city, we could hardly wait to ask, "Did you know her, Peter?"

"I don't know. How can I know? We have many Indonesian nurses in Holland. But this one—she gets me all mixed up."

I had placed Peter's painting "Mur Woods" on a stand in my apartment to study it more closely and to let Vera see it. Vera was thoroughly familiar with Peter's story. She was transcribing all of our tapes. She already knew about the boy's face in the clouds and the man with the beard. As soon as she looked at the painting she saw them, as plainly as I did—and without my pointing them out to her. She agreed that the child's face looked like Gloria Ann.

"Or Peter when he was a little boy," she suggested. She was reading my mind.

She suddenly startled me with a small scream. "Oh, no . . . ! Look at it this way. . . . Do you see what I see? Or am I crazy . . . ? *Something* is wrong with that man!"

She was staring wide-eyed, as though seeing a ghost. Then I saw it, too. I turned away, engulfed in a sickening wave of emotion. What a tortured man Peter was! My heart ached for him. For the first time I was actually frightened. And with the fear was an utter sense of futility. I was too deep into a psychic world that I could never understand or explain.

There was another face in the clouds that both of us recognized immediately.

It was the face of a dog with his head thrown back, his eyes turned upward, foam pouring from his mouth. Above him was the man with the beard. The foam coming out of the dog's mouth swirled into the man's beard!

Vera said, "We can't both be crazy, can we?"

"I don't know."

"Do you think you should show it to Peter?"

"I don't know." I was still in a state of shock.

Later we searched "Mur Woods" upside down, sideways, and from every angle of light to try to find other hidden images in the cloud conformations. We asked dozens of friends what they saw in the painting. The answers were always the same: the three faces . . . the child, the man with the beard, and the dog. It was obvious that they had not been painted intentionally. There was no distinct shape or outline, though they could be seen distinctly and clearly in the formation of clouds, the blend of light, shadows, and darkness.

Why did it have to be a dog? we asked. Why couldn't it have been something else—a bird or a unicorn?

Why did "Mur Woods" reveal those three specific psychic images so clearly—the boy's face that looked like Gloria Ann, the man with the beard from the other world, and his dog, Tommy?

Can anyone believe this was sheer coincidence?

It was not Peter's conscious self painting "Mur Woods," of

that I was convinced. Just as I knew that Ana Kaneel was not sent here to interrupt our lives without purpose.

There may never be a scientific explanation for Peter's psychic painting of "Mur Woods" but I am willing to accept the word of anthropologists who report that in some primitive tribes there are certain individuals capable of producing a state of trance and mental dissociation which is interpreted as "spirit possession." What spirit possession had control of Peter's hands and fingers while he was painting "Mur Woods"?

Vera and I took "Mur Woods" with us when we went to see Ana Kaneel.

She immediately saw the little boy with his face in the clouds and said, "That's Peter, when he was a child."

She saw the man with the beard and said, strangely, "I somehow associate a voice with him. He may be one of Peter's guides." (We had not told her anything about this book or its contents.)

She saw the dog's face instantly and said, "Look at the eyes. They're so sad. He looks as though he is drowning." She paused, thoughtfully, then added, "This painting is very Salvador-Dali-ish. It was done by a man of inmost suffering."

"It was done by Peter."

"Yes, I know." (Though we hadn't told her.)

She wheeled her teacart out to the patio and then went in to find Peter's painting. She had told me on the phone that she had located it and of course she would be delighted to let me see it.

She returned with a small (six-by-eight) print of a black and white pencil sketch of two deer.

"This isn't Peter's," I said, handing it back to her. I assumed she had merely picked up the wrong picture by mistake, without looking.

She surprised me by saying, "Oh, yes, this is one of his early paintings—when he first started."

"It couldn't be. This isn't the way Peter paints," I said.

"And this isn't Peter's signature," Vera added, pointing to the tiny, almost illegible signature in the left-hand corner.

"Yes, that was the way he signed his early paintings."

"But that isn't his name. It's not Peter Hurkos."

"No. That was the name he used then."

We held the picture up to the light, studied the signature closely, and deciphered the delicate pinpoint-printed name as H. Van Meegeren.

"He's a famous Dutch painter," said Ana. "He was insane. He died in prison. The original of this painting is in a museum in Amsterdam. This is an exact replica. Peter signed all his early paintings with that name."

"I'm sorry but I don't believe it," I said. "Peter could never write like that. And he could never spell that name the same way twice."

Vera added politely, "And this is not a painting. It's a print."

"Yes, a copy," said Ana. "But he copied it from one of his own paintings."

"From where?"

"From something he drew on the sheets, the pillowcases."

"Did you see him drawing this picture on the sheets or pillow-cases?" I asked.

"No."

"Did you see him making this copy?"

"No. Maybe it was a photograph."

"It is not a photograph. And it is not an original copy of anything. It is a print," we told her.

She was unruffled, impassive, impervious to our objections. "But Peter told me he painted it for me and so I had it framed. I treasure it because Peter gave it to me. . . ."

"If Peter gave it to you, why is this inscription on the back of it?"

In very fine delicate handwriting were the words "The deer . . . Faithful, upright, swift and pure . . . A token of my sincere love . . . La Nina."

"Who was La Nina?"

"Oh, she was just a patient of mine, a little ten-year-old girl."

The handwriting definitely was not that of any ten-year-old child.

What Ana Kaneel's motive was we simply could not fathom.

I asked if I could borrow the print and take it to Peter to psychometrize.

"Of course," she said, which only compounded the puzzlement. If it was not Peter's work, why would she permit me to show it to him?

I didn't tell Peter or Stephy or Tess that I had been to see Ana Kaneel again. They did not know about the picture.

"Have you ever seen this picture before, Peter?"

"No."

"Have you ever painted a picture like this?"

"No. This is not my style."

"You're sure you never saw this picture before?"

"Well, I have seen animals like this in a movie. I think a movie from Africa. Beautiful animals . . ."

"You remember the Indonesian nurse we went to see? She says this is the picture you gave her."

"This is not mine. It is not a painting anyway. And I sign all my paintings Peter Hurkos. Where is Peter Hurkos on here?"

"She said this is the way you signed your name on your early paintings, Peter. Can you recognize this?"

"Are you kidding? I could never write so small. I can't read it. What is the name?"

I didn't tell him the name. Not that it would have made any difference. I asked him to psychometrize the picture and tell me what he saw.

"I see Dutch," he said. "This person passed away very strange . . . very strange. . . . He is in a room where he couldn't get out, like a jail. . . . Lot of stolen stuff . . . stolen stuff. . . . This is not the only drawing. . . . I see oil paintings. . . . Person is much better in his own field, in oils. . . . Big trouble with Germans. . . . I see him with Germans involved, dealing with Ger-

mans. . . . And he's in a room where he couldn't get out. . . .
Death in the room with walls all around. . . ."

That was enough. I told him to stop. I was ready to scream at
this whole psychic idiocy! In my notebook was the biography of
Han Van Meegeren (1889–1947) copied from The New International Illustrated Encyclopedia of Art.

Van Meegeren was a famous forger of paintings, especially Vermeers.

"What is a forger?" Peter asked.

I tried to explain. Then I read excerpts from my notes:

. . . Art critics did not favor his work, and Van Meegeren could
not take their criticism. He decided to retaliate by proving that they
knew nothing of art, and judged artists only by their past reputa-
tions. He decided to make fools of them all, by painting a work of
Vermeer, and when it was acclaimed as a magnificent original by the
master, he would expose himself as the artist. . . .

. . . His first work ("Christ at Emmaus") was hailed as a master-
piece and purchased by a museum in Rotterdam for about
$378,000. Though the forger had set out to make a point about the
critics, he changed his mind when he received the check. Once this
first work was accepted, the rest followed in quick succession. . . .
In 1945, he was arrested on a charge of collaborating with the Germans, and evidence existed that he had been involved in the sale of
a Vermeer painting to the Nazi leader Hermann Goering, for about
$792,000. . . .

"Oh, my God, a lot of money for a painting," Peter com-
mented.

Stephy asked, "If people paid him so much money for his paintings, why did he have to go to jail?"

Neither of them seemed to understand the word "forger" as applied to an artist. I explained that the artist had painted in the
exact style of another Dutch painter, Vermeer, signed his paintings with Vermeer's name, and passed them off as newly discovered "Vermeers." That is known as forgery, I said, and Van
Meegeren was known as a forger.

"Do you understand now?" I asked.

"Yes, I understand now forger. But why wouldn't he sign his

own name? I could copy anything I want to copy—clouds, trees, flowers, anything. But I always sign my own name, Peter Hurkos." He looked at the small print again and said, "This is not my name. How do you think I sign that name? I don't even know the man. Who is he?"

"That's the man I was just telling you about, the forger. His name is Van Meegeren."

"Never heard of him."

"Peter, what were you talking to the Indonesian nurse about in Dutch—out there in the garden?"

"Nothing. How she knew me from the hospital. . . ."

"Did you tell her that she was going to die in a plane crash over Buenos Aires?"

He exploded, in a rage. "Are you crazy? You know I never tell people if they are going to die. That woman is crazy, belongs in a mental hospital. I never saw her before. I never saw this picture before. She calls me a forger, now she says I tell her she will die in a plane crash! . . . Leave me alone. Don't ask me any more questions!"

"Just one more, Peter. Do you remember being in the Zuidwal Hospital again, a second time—a few years after your fall?"

"No. Never. I was there many times, yes, for check-ups in the clinic. But they did not keep me again as a patient."

We checked it out. There are no records of Peter being admitted as a patient at the Zuidwal Hospital a second time, no records that he was ever under observation for "seizures" or symptoms of epilepsy, no records of two Spanish doctors boring holes in his skull to relieve pressure on his brain.

According to his brother and sister, still living in Holland, Peter returned to the Zuidwal clinic from time to time after his fall, but always as an outpatient. According to the records that were sent to us, the only time he was hospitalized as a patient was during that period immediately after his fall, from July 10 to August 5, 1941.

What was the meaning and motive behind Ana Kaneel's strange story? Was she simply mistaken, or hallucinating? Did she perhaps have a memory block of her own? Why did she tell us the little Van Meegeren print was Peter's painting? Did she know that Van Meegeren was a forger, or was this another in the endless eerie chain of psychic "coincidences" that always seemed to surround Peter?

Who was Ana Kaneel? Where did she come from? She had materialized as mysteriously as the three faces in the psychic painting "Mur Woods."

As I said in the beginning, I am not a mystic, I don't believe in these things, and I cannot explain them. But they happened. Maybe it was the opening of my own "third eye." Somehow I knew that the mysteries locked within Ana Kaneel and "Mur Woods" held the answer to Peter's soul-searching question: "Who am I?"

{20}

The Search Ends

I HAD LONG SINCE ABANDONED MY SEARCH FOR A PICTURE TO match the face of the boy in the clouds. Except one—Peter's.

I already knew who he was before Ana Kaneel told me. I had known it from that day when I first recognized Gloria Ann as the face in "Mur Woods." She was sitting in her highchair, her head tilted to one side listening to us, her big brown eyes regarding us with a quizzical expression, her face framed in black curly hair.

She was almost an exact replica of the little boy's face in the clouds. Almost. She was still a baby. The little boy could have been ten or twelve. But with a white chiffon scarf around her neck, like the little boy's floating cravat of clouds, she could have been the child Peter subconsciously painted in "Mur Woods." But she hadn't even been born yet.

I asked myself, Why, why, why? It was one of the many unanswered whys about Peter.

He had painted the picture while Stephy was pregnant with Gloria Ann.

He had painted it especially for her, and it was the one picture in the house that belonged to Stephy as her very own. She treasured it because it was hers alone, but she did not recognize the child's face as Gloria Ann's—or Peter's—until I mentioned it.

Peter had always said the boy's face was the man with the beard as a child, and Stephy had accepted this without questioning, without looking for any more symbolisms.

When I pointed out the resemblance to her own child, she looked at the face in the clouds again and exclaimed, "Why, of course it's Gloria Ann. It's exactly the way she looks now—with all that curly hair and Peter's eyes."

Peter had gone into another room to rest. He was tired and he was nearing the end of his patience with our questions. Besides, there were certain matters I wanted to discuss with Stephy and Tess without him.

"Let's go back now and try to remember everything you can about how he happened to paint this picture," I said.

"He had just finished working on a case in San Francisco, and we had gone down to this place, Mur [Muir] Woods, so he could rest. It was a beautiful place," Stephy recalled. "It's where all the redwoods are. Peter likes to walk in the woods, you know, so we went walking among the redwoods. I don't know what happened to him. I guess he saw something like what he's always seeing in that other world he keeps talking about.

"He told me he saw a light up there in front of us, and he had to go and find something. I thought he meant that whatever he saw had something to do with the case he was working on. Anyway I didn't see any light but Peter started walking fast and faster, and he just went off and left me," Stephy said.

"When he came back, I asked him if he had found anything. He said no. He seemed upset about something so I told him to look at these beautiful redwood trees all around us. I asked him if he would do a painting of the redwoods for me, and he said sure, okay, and this is what he painted.

"I named it 'Mur Woods' because that's the name of the place where we were and it was so beautiful that I wanted something to remember it by. And we didn't see that boy's face or the man with the beard until later, after someone pointed them out to us, and I had already named it. I still like 'Mur Woods.' But do you notice something? He didn't paint the redwoods. Those aren't redwood trees. It's all dark there where the redwoods are supposed to be. And there weren't any clouds like that, either. Or any light up ahead of us. But that's the way Peter saw it in his mind."

To any casual observer and from almost any angle "Mur Woods" is only a painting of a pathway leading through darkness and clouds, up and upward toward the light.

"It's a symbolic painting," Tess explained. "I think all of Peter's paintings are symbolic and psychic, but this is the only one that has those faces in it."

I asked them to bring out all the photographs they could find of Peter as a baby or a young boy, as well as pictures of Gloria Ann.

It was as I suspected—the baby pictures of Peter and Gloria Ann were almost identical.

And we found what I knew we would find—some old photographs of the Van der Hurk family showing the boy Pieter with a thick mop of black curly hair and the face of the boy in the clouds.

Both Stephy and Tess noticed the similarity immediately. I didn't have to tell them.

"Look!" Stephy said. "Their hair is even parted on the same side [the left side]. . . . But if that's Peter, then who is the man with the beard?"

"Let me show you something else," I said, cautiously. I tilted the picture slightly, at a certain angle, and asked, "Do you see anything else?"

Tess said quietly, "Yes, I see it." She was ashen.

When Stephy saw it, she recoiled, then reached for the picture. She glowered at me, as though it were my fault, and said sharply, "You can't show that to Peter!"

At this moment Peter walked into the room.

"What's wrong now?" he asked. "What are you doing here

with my painting? Don't ask me any more questions, I don't want to talk about it. I already have told you everything I know a hundred times. Stephy, go put that painting back in the bedroom where it belongs. Thank God, I go to India tomorrow."

His passport lay on the table. He was leaving for India to work on a new case. His mind was on the trip.

But I had to know his own answers to "Mur Woods."

I tried to cajole him by saying, "We're not really working now, Peter. We were just looking at the painting again because it's so beautiful."

"Ya, beautiful woods. . . . Tess, turn that damn thing off. We work no more today." Tess turned off the tape recorder—but turned it on again when he wasn't looking.

"Peter, you know what we've decided? That little boy's face you painted looks like Gloria Ann." I thought that might please him. It worked.

"Oh, ya?" His eyes brightened and his face beamed. "Let me see it again," he said.

We stood the painting up on a counter behind Gloria Ann, who as usual was observing all the proceedings from her highchair.

"Wait a minute," said Stephy. "I want to show you something." She ran into another room and came back with a white scarf which she draped around the baby's neck.

"I see it! I see it!" Peter cried. He was as excited as a child with a new toy. He jumped up from the table, went over and lifted Gloria Ann from her highchair, and whirled her above his head. "That's my baby, my baby. Did you know papa painted your picture?" he cooed. He smothered her with kisses, then put her down.

He stepped back and looked at the painting again. His face suddenly clouded.

"No, it can't be Gloria Ann," he said. "She was not even born yet. How can it be a baby who is not even born . . . ? No, I tell you that is the man with the beard when he was a child."

He was very definite about it.

"But the little boy also looks exactly like you, Peter, when you were a child. Here, look at these photographs. . . ."

We showed him the pictures of the Van der Hurk family. He hadn't looked at them in a long time. He seemed delighted to see them again. He would point his finger at himself in the family groups, or sometimes alone, and say, "There, that is Pieter van der Hurk when he was a boy. . . . You see? That is what Pieter van der Hurk looked like. . . . That is the person who got left down here when I went to the other world, and he never came back in my body."

He spoke of Pieter van der Hurk in the third person as though he were a totally separate being.

He compared the pictures of Pieter van der Hurk and Gloria Ann which we showed him. He smiled and said, "Yes. The same. Identical."

We compared the childhood pictures of Pieter van der Hurk with the boy's face in the clouds and I asked, "Do you see the resemblance?"

"Yes. Sure. Identical."

"Don't you think the boy's face could be you as a child, Pieter van der Hurk?"

He hesitated a long time, thinking about it. "Could be . . . I don't know. . . . My hands just went. But how could I paint myself without knowing it? I'm confused. Now you get me all mixed up. . . ."

He paused, with a puzzled expression on his face, then asked, "But if that is Pieter van der Hurk, then who would be the man with the beard?"

A good question. With no answer.

"No . . . no . . . no . . ." he said slowly. "That is not Pieter van der Hurk. It is somebody else I don't know, somebody from the many lives they give me in the other world. . . .

"The man with the beard," he said. His voice was a whisper. His dark, brooding eyes were focused now on the "Mur Woods" painting. I was watching him closely. I saw his eyes move from the boy's face toward the bearded figure in the upper left-hand corner. I saw the slight sudden twitch of his head and the trancelike look that came into his eyes. His body stiffened. His haggard, haunted face was distorted in anguish. I knew what he was seeing.

"Oh, my God!" he cried. "It's Tommy . . . my dog Tommy
. . . when he is drowning. . . . His eyes looking up at me . . .
the foam from his mouth. . . . Take it away! . . . Why do they
do this to me?"

He dropped his head in his hands, choking back the sobbing inside of him, crying out in a voice from the grave, to someone who
wasn't there, "Why do you do this to me? Why don't you leave
me alone? Why do you punish me so long? Why don't you let me
come back and have peace? . . . Why? . . . Why? . . ."

He raised his head and looked at us, without seeing us. Then he
got up and left the room.

"I told you not to show it to him," Stephy said quietly.

"I didn't show it to him. He saw it himself. I was hoping he
wouldn't see it."

"But you must have turned the picture a certain way, just a little."

"She didn't have to do that," said Tess. "When these things
come to Peter, they just come, and there's no way you can stop
them."

"But I don't understand those men up there at all," said
Stephy. "Here they give him all of these gifts—his psychic gift,
and his music and painting. Why does he still have to be
punished for something he did when he was only eleven years
old?"

"I think the punishment is just in Peter's mind," said Tess.

"What I'd like to know," I said, "is what happened to the
Pieter van der Hurk who left his body during his fall in 1941.
This is what seems to haunt Peter. And who is the somebody else
who came back in his body?"

Stephy went into the other room to see how Peter was feeling.

When she returned, she said, "Peter asked me to tell you that
he doesn't want to discuss any of this ever again. Ever. With you
or anyone else. He doesn't want any more questions. He feels better now. But he says the book is finished. He doesn't even want to
read it or hear about it. He wants to forget it."

{21}

Epilogue: Who Is Ana Kaneel?

PETER DIDN'T WANT TO HEAR ABOUT MY LAST SESSION WITH ANA Kaneel. It was just as well.

I knew my question about the voice had frightened her and that there was something she wanted to tell me.

I asked again, "Did Peter ever tell you about hearing a voice?"

This time she surprised me by replying calmly, "He did not have to tell me. I heard it myself. Many times."

"*You* heard the voice, too?"

"Yes. It was the voice of the mediator, the one who translates, the spirit guide. It was another voice coming out of Peter's mouth. I remember the first time I heard it," she said. "I entered his room one evening to test his neuro-reflexes. Everything was normal except his eyes. I pointed the flashlight in them. His pupils contracted but he swiftly moved away and looked aside as if seeing someone, listening to someone. Then he began speaking in this strange high-pitched voice. It was like a second image, another person coming out of his body.

"The voice had an accent. It was someone from the Eastern world—Persia or India, I thought. I had never heard an Indian accent at that time. Since then I have been in India and Persia and I am certain the voice of the mediator was from the east coast of India, probably Bombay.

"Peter spoke in Dutch, of course. But then the other voice would come in this singsong dialect, and Peter would look aside as though listening. He never expressed himself without looking in a different direction."

"Do you remember anything this other voice said?"

"Of course. How could I forget? Peter said to me that he does not believe he came out of his mother's womb. That was the first thing that frightened me. It was the other person speaking through him. His body was being used by somebody else, like a receiving and broadcasting station, by a person who wanted to get this message across. Why would anyone want to tell Peter that he did not come out of his mother's womb?

"I come from an oriental culture. . . . We are very close to death. . . . We are taught from an early age that death is part of life. We are taught to talk to those who are about to die and those who have come back from near dying, like Peter. He had been through a transcendental experience and I was in awe of him. I felt something emanating from him, like a source of energy. I had a closer rapport with him than some of the nurses did. We could communicate without saying a word. I knew that he had died and was reborn. I knew that his body was just a shell, invaded by a living soul. I could understand all of this intellectually, but emotionally I was not prepared for those strange voices speaking in many tongues and saying so many things that frightened me.

"I felt drawn toward this man whose eyes were always vacant, who seemed still to be in another world. But I always had a certain fear when I went into his room. I don't know why. It was the kind of fear you have when you meet someone, a perfect stranger, and you suddenly realize—it could have been someone you met in another life. . . . I felt he knew too much about me. . . . I didn't want to have anything to do with him . . . as little as possible. . . . Still I had to take care of him. He was my patient."

"Why was it so urgent for you to see Peter again after all these years?" I asked.

"I will tell you why. I have never told this to anyone else—except Peter, when we met again the other night. I was straightening his pillow and placed my hand on his forehead. He was burning with fever. He grabbed my wrist and the other high-pitched voice cried out, 'Fire, explosion, be careful!' But that isn't all. He told me exactly when and where I was going to die. He said at the age of fifty I would die in a plane crash over Buenos Aires. He even gave me the exact date—April 27, 1980. That is only five years away. Do you think knowing this has been easy to live with?

"I was only a teen-ager then, and I was terrified. When I became twenty-five I was petrified. I thought, I am not ready to die in twenty-five years. . . . I have lived with this for all these years. I remember standing there transfixed and terrified, listening to the strange voice of this man telling me I was going to die in a plane crash. In spite of my oriental culture, I discovered that I really wasn't very well acquainted with death, and I was not prepared for living with that fear for so many years.

"Everything else he told me has happened exactly as he said it would. So now you must understand why I desperately wanted to see him again. I wanted to know if this was the same person who talked to me at that time, who told me these things that have affected and changed my whole life. Was he the same patient I had at the Zuidwal? Would he still say that I am going to die in a plane crash over Buenos Aires in five years?"

"Was he the same patient you had in the hospital?"

"Yes, physically it was the same man. But he told me that he was not the same person who said I would die in a plane crash, that I must be mistaken and it must have been somebody else. He told me this when we were in the garden and speaking in Dutch. He said I definitely am not going to die in a plane crash and that

I am going to live longer than five years. But even if it does happen in five years, I am ready to go now. I am prepared. Peter has enriched my life in many ways by telling me those things when I was very young," said Ana. "But by the same token he has become very poor."

"What do you mean by that?"

"His body has been used so long for other purposes, by other people who have entered it, exploited it, possessed it, that he is completely drained and exhausted," she said. "You can see the exhaustion that lies around his eyes and his mouth. I feel sorry for this man I met again the other night. I recognized the loneliness in him immediately . . . the loneliness, the sorrow, and the anguish. . . .

"I don't know how long his body has been used. But I do know that he doesn't even possess it, he has nothing to say about it. I am sure some of the people who entered his body were good spirits, but there were evil spirits also. I have often wondered who was using Peter's body as an instrument to tell me that I would die. Who wanted me dead? Who wanted to use my body?

"I am sorry this has caused me to dislike people from India. I have never had an aversion to any race of people before, but I am certain this was an evil spirit who possessed Peter's body."

"Did you hear other voices besides this one coming out of Peter?"

"Yes. There were many. But this was the dominant one, from the Eastern world. He was using Peter's body for evil purposes. . . . I wasn't the only one. . . . There were others affected by it. . . ." She hesitated.

"Did you ever hear about anyone who came into Peter's room and tried to kill him, suffocate him with a pillow?" I asked.

"Yes," she said in a resigned tone, as though she knew I was going to ask that question. Nurse Zelda had reported it to the hospital officials.

"It was one of the nurses," said Ana. "She was so upset and depressed that she committed suicide over it. But she wasn't trying to kill Peter. It was the spirit possession using his body for an evil purpose.

"Every time she went into Peter's room to bring him messages or flowers, his breathing would become hard and labored, and he would tell her that she was suffocating him, taking his oxygen away. When she moved close to him to try to straighten his pillow, he would become panicky. He thought she was trying to smother him with the pillow.

"The poor girl was frightened out of her wits. But Peter did not know. . . . It was the spirit possession of his body."

"Do you think he is still possessed by these same evil spirits?"

"I don't know if they are the same. But his body has been used for so long as a receiving and broadcasting station by others that his energy source is completely drained, depleted. When I first knew him in Holland, he wasn't really a person, he was a patient, and when I would look at him his eyes were vacant. Now I have met him for the first time as a person and his eyes are not vacant —but they are agonized with loneliness and suffering.

"He enriched my life by telling me that I was going to die. I had to face death. I had to overcome my fear of death—and flying. I learned to fly; I even have my pilot's license because of Peter Hurkos! He changed my life in so many ways. I went to Paris and studied transcendental meditation and parapsychology, trying to find answers to my strange experience with Peter. Psychic phenomena is something that cannot be explained scientifically. But in my search for answers, I grew—and Peter has deteriorated.

"He has become more involved with this world, more misunderstood, he has no mental communication with any other human being. The mental loneliness of this man is pitiful. He is like a drowning man grasping for something, screaming for help, and if he doesn't get help I don't know what will happen to him.

"He needs to go to some remote place and become completely alone and recharge his batteries. . . . He must be on top of a mountain and cleanse himself. I have seen this in my dreams and I have learned it through transcendental meditation. . . . There is a strange feeling I have about this man. . . . Could it have been that we met in another life? No . . . no . . . I met him in the Zuidwal Hospital."

I asked her about the "Mur Woods" painting again. She remembered the boy's face, the bearded figure, and the dog.

"I told you that painting was done by a man of inmost suffering. He is a man drowning like that dog was drowning."

"Did he ever talk to you about a dog?" I interrupted.

"No, no, I am speaking symbolically. I could feel it in the vibrations, the aura from the painting. There is the look of anguish in the bearded figure's face that is the same as in Peter's . . . and I still associate that face with a voice. . . . No, I don't think it's that voice from the Eastern world that possessed his body while he was in the hospital. . . . It is more like many voices from many other lives. . . . I can't be sure. . . ."

But she was sure of one thing—that the little boy's face was Peter as a child.

"And you will notice it is the only part of the painting that is calm and peaceful and tranquil. That is what Peter would like to be, and it is the state of being he must return to—a little child. This painting literally screams at you from Peter's gut, from his insides. . . . Someone must do something for this man. . . ."

What a strange and incredible outpouring from one who had crossed our paths so briefly but whose own life had been haunted by Peter Hurkos almost from the time he returned to this world.

I was still sure that Ana Kaneel had been sent into our lives for a purpose, though it was difficult to figure out what the purpose was.

I returned once more to the small print of the two deer which she said Peter had given her.

"Did you know that the artist Van Meegeren was a famous forger?"

"No. Really? . . . Well, one never knows who we might meet in another life."

"Peter says he never saw that picture before, he doesn't know how you got it, but he didn't give it to you," I said.

"Well, then it could have been from a person he met in another life who was using his body. . . . He has a memory block in many areas. . . ."

Did Ana Kaneel have a memory block of her own? Or was she, too, a reincarnated spirit from another world?

By all accounts it was the missing nurse Zelda who had been the closest to Peter in the hospital, who knew about the voices he heard and the evil spirits who took control of his body. It was nurse Zelda who fled from his room in terror and reported the incident of the "big fire and explosion" to her supervisors, though she apparently kept the details to herself. None of our contacts in Holland had heard anything about his prediction that one of the Zuidwal nurses would be killed in a plane crash over Buenos Aires. This was odd, since most of his predictions, even the minor ones, were well circulated and eventually became well publicized.

It was nurse Zelda who was so concerned over Peter's feeling of being suffocated when another nurse came into the room, and his fixation that she was trying to kill him. Zelda also reported this to her supervisors.

Ana Kaneel insists that she had Peter as a patient at the Zuidwal after the war, in 1948 or 1949, when he was hospitalized a second time. Yet, there are no records for a second hospitalization. In virtually all details Ana's story would indicate that she must be mistaken in her dates, that she was indeed Peter's nurse in those weeks of July and August 1941, following his accident.

She had described many incidents and circumstances relating to Peter that checked out with accounts from others and could only be known by those familiar with Peter's case at that time—after his fall.

Completely mystifying, however, was that brain operation by two Spanish brain surgeons which Ana had mentioned.

And who was the nurse who committed suicide?

Most puzzling of all was Ana's relationship with or to nurse Zelda. If Zelda was head nurse on Peter's floor and Ana an assistant head nurse, they must have worked together with Peter. Yet, Ana seemed barely to know Zelda, and never mentioned her name unless it was brought up. I said to her once, "You must have known nurse Zelda?"

"Oh, yes."

"What was she like?"

"A very fine woman." Then she changed the subject and I didn't pursue it.

Certain details of Ana's story would almost positively identify her as nurse Zelda. But why would she deny it?

I was ready to pass on that question and simply accept the fact that Ana and nurse Zelda were one and the same and that Ana had her own personal reasons for not wanting her identity known.

This could have been one of the few comparatively simple answers, I thought, in the whole complex mystical mishmash.

It was not meant to be.

I began comparing dates. Peter had told Ana that she would die in the plane crash in 1980, at the age of fifty. Unlike most women, Ana did not mind revealing her age. In fact, she was obsessed by it. She had been counting the years for a long time.

"I am forty-five now and I have only five more years to live," she had told me.

If Ana Kaneel becomes fifty years old in 1980, she was born in 1930. She could not have been nurse Zelda, nor an assistant head nurse to Zelda, nor even a nurse's aide in the Zuidwal in 1941. She would have been only eleven years old.

She was a teen-ager, she said, when she had Peter as her patient in 1948 or 1949, the time she remembers as his re-entry into the world of consciousness. But there are no records, no memories from anyone but Ana of her strange psychic journey with Peter.

How could she know so much about him?

There is only her answer.

"It could be that I have known him in another life. . . . But I am sure that I met him at the Zuidwal."

Appendix:
The Sharon Tate Murders

ALTHOUGH PETER HAD BEEN UNIMPRESSED WITH THE PREDICTIONS of Nostradamus, especially the one concerning his own future, nevertheless his recognition in this world was to come primarily from his work on criminal cases.

"I will stay beside you. I will be with you. I will give you the insight and the vision like mine," Nostradamus had said.

Curiously, while reading about Nostradamus later, I came across some words that could have been written for Peter, they described him so precisely.

> . . . He occasionally received actual names—sometimes correctly, but usually disguised or distorted. . . . It is as though he might have entered a trancelike state and by automatic writing or immediately after emerging wrote Latin phrases. . . . He obtained messages by semisuspension of consciousness . . . drew upon hidden controls of

his unconscious and obtained artificially a condition of auto-hypnosis. . . .

I have seen Peter receive actual names, sometimes correctly, sometimes disguised or distorted. I have seen him in a trancelike state do "automatic writing," but more often "automatic" pictures. And I have watched him thousands of times as he obtained "messages" by "semisuspension of consciousness."

But of course none of this is admissible as evidence in a criminal case.

As Vincent Bugliosi pointed out in his book *Helter Skelter: The True Story of the Manson Murders* (Norton, 1974), referring to Peter's work on this case, ". . . those in law enforcement have a standard procedure for handling such 'information': listen politely, then forget it. Being inadmissible as evidence, it is valueless."

It may be valueless as evidence in a murder case, but it should not be valueless to anyone exploring the nature of man's mind, for Peter's psychic vision and insight in the case of the Sharon Tate murders, as they were called, would seem strong evidence that the mind is indeed capable of certain supersensory perceptions that are presently beyond man's understanding.

I was with Peter during his work on the Sharon Tate murders, one of the most baffling and horrifying murder cases in the annals of crime. And I believe that if the LAPD (Los Angeles Police Department) had done more than "listen politely, then forget it," the case might have been solved sooner. Within two weeks after Peter started working on the case, he was abruptly dismissed. Why? Did he know too much? I am not so sure the police didn't listen to him. Although they would never admit it, the evidence that Peter turned over to them might have helped in the capture and conviction of Charles Manson and his co-conspirators.

One thing I know for certain: it could have.

As Dr. F. Regis Riesenman once told me, Peter's best work is done on criminal cases, especially murders and missing people. Many of these, including the Boston Strangler case, the case of the missing Jim Thompson and the Ann Arbor/Ypsilanti coed murders, were related in my book *The Psychic World of Peter Hurkos.*

We have been primarily concerned in this book with the search for Peter's identity, his other self, from clues provided by his out-of-body experience in that other world. But I believe his work on the Sharon Tate murders should be included, at least as an appendix, because it illustrates Peter's psychic gift at its best. Moreover, now that the verdict is in and the Bugliosi book has been written, revealing many details that were not brought out during the Manson trial, it is possible to compare those details with my own notes and transcriptions made while Peter was working on the case.

Bugliosi was the prosecutor in the Manson trial, the longest trial in American history, and his book, *Helter Skelter*, is voluminously documented, as well as totally enthralling to anyone who likes gory murder mysteries.

Fortunately, I have kept my own voluminous notebooks on the Tate case and the original tapes we made with Roman Polanski (Sharon Tate's husband) and others—in the death house and elsewhere.

I should like to emphasize that my notebooks, kept in daily-diary form as Peter worked on the case, were dated from Tuesday, August 12, 1969, the day Peter began working on the case and only three days after the grisly murders occurred, through August 20, when he was dropped from the case. This was long before the Manson gang surfaced in the headlines.

I reread my own notes with disbelief. I had forgotten how accurate Peter had been.

On the very first page of my notebook (Tate, No. 1) are scribbled the words "Small, little man with beard . . . Charlie . . . only about five-foot-six. [He missed by four inches. Charles Manson is diminutive, only five-foot-two.] . . . And another skinny person, tall . . . Charlie, Charlie . . . I keep seeing Charlie. . . . [Charles "Tex" Watson and two of the Manson Family females actually executed the murders, masterminded by Manson, according to Bugliosi. Charles Watson was tall and skinny, six-foot-one.] Small little car, Ford type [correct] . . . David . . . I see David . . . Charlie . . . Billy . . . Sally. . . ."

Throughout all my notes these were the names that kept recurring—Charlie more than any other, also David, Billy, and Sally.

Common enough names, to be sure, but he could have thrown in others, such as a Joe or Tom or Al or Dick. He didn't. Nowhere in my notes is there any mention of other names he saw involved in the brutal killings. As it turned out, there was no David involved in the murders, but among the ten females and three males later arrested at the Barker Ranch near Death Valley (in November 1969) were Charles Manson, David Lee Hamic (also known as Bill Vance, an ex-con with more aliases than Manson), and Susan Atkins, Sandra Good, and Sherry Andrews, any one of whom might have been the Sally in Peter's mind.

From the beginning he insisted on several points which later turned out to be accurate: that the murders were committed by a gang, a ritualistic cult that included both men and women, and were involved in sex and narcotics; that three people had entered the Tate-Polanski home while one remained outside; that the murderers knew Sharon Tate and the layout of the grounds because they had been there before; that the leader of the gang or cult was "a small man who thinks he is Jesus Christ, and has been in trouble with the police already [Manson had spent half his life in institutions] . . . he looks like a farmer but is not a farmer . . . very sadistic . . . crazy nut, tough, hard, and vulgar. . . ."

Peter also said that the victims were caught unaware. . . . "Nobody suspicious about killing because they thought he was a friend . . ."; that the guy (Voytek Frykowski) was the first to be killed; Jay Sebring was second and Sharon Tate last; and that the case would involve many "high up" Hollywood and show-business people. This could certainly be considered the psychic understatement of all time, considering the number of top-name celebrities paraded across the pages of *Helter Skelter*, including those who had formerly lived in the Tate-Polanski home in Benedict Canyon (Candice Bergen and Doris Day's son, Terry Melcher, and the Henry Fondas); the celebrities who had visited there (Lee Marvin had once said, "This house spooks me."); special friends of the Polanskis and/or Jay Sebring (Paul Newman, Steve McQueen, Cass Elliot, John and Michelle Phillips of the Mamas and Papas rock group, and some of the Beach Boys); and Manson's "death list" of celebrities whom he had planned to exterminate (Elizabeth Taylor, Frank Sinatra, Tom Jones, Steve McQueen).

And Peter had described to me, rather accurately, the inside of the rambling ranch-type death house (the newspapers had printed pictures of the outside), with special emphasis on the open loft and wooden beams. "I see something wrong on the wood above, the beams . . ." he said. Among other things the bodies of Sharon Tate and Jay Sebring, her former lover, were tied together with a nylon rope looped over one of the beams.

The details of the mass murders have been well publicized. To recap briefly, the five victims were actress Sharon Tate (one of the stars in *Valley of the Dolls*), eight months pregnant; Jay Sebring, famous Hollywood men's hair stylist and once Sharon's fiancé; Voytek Frykowski, Polish refugee and friend of Polanski's; his girl friend, Abigail Folger, a Radcliffe graduate and heiress to the Folger coffee fortune; and Steve Parent, eighteen, a student and friend of the caretaker who lived in the guest house on the property. Parent had been shot to death in his car in the driveway as he was about to leave.

I heard the news broadcast of the murders on my car radio in Palm Springs on the morning of August 9, 1969.

I had more than passing interest in it because I had known both Sharon Tate and Jay Sebring, as well as Roman Polanski. I first met Sharon when she was making a movie for television called *Don't Make Waves*. (I had a small role in it as a reporter.) She had been to my home many times to pose for pictures for my husband. The last time I saw her was on a six-day cruise to Acapulco for a shipboard premiere of the movie version of Jacqueline Susann's best-selling book, *Valley of the Dolls*.

I don't remember whether it was Jay Sebring or Roman Polanski with whom she was in love at the time. I knew her through both of them. "Roman is such a beautiful human being," Sharon once told me. "Sometimes things are difficult, sometimes good. But it makes life twice as interesting."

Sharon was not only a beautiful girl, but there was a sad, haunting, ethereal quality about her. She was well mannered, gentle, soft-spoken, and sensitive, essentially shy, very unlike the typical exhibitionist Hollywood sex pot. But she impressed me as a girl who could be easily led, controlled, molded, and manipulated by the man she loved. This is verified in some detail in the Bugliosi book, with regard to both Jay Sebring and Roman Polanski.

Peter was brought into the case by an attorney named Peter Knecht, who had been Jay Sebring's lawyer and was also a personal friend of Sebring's.

From the very beginning, Peter Hurkos had told me that the death house—which Sharon often called her "love house"—had been the scene of frequent sex and drug orgies and black magic rituals in which all the occupants of the house—as well as many other invited guests—had participated. Soon after the mass murders, a neighbor was heard to comment, "Live freaky, die freaky"—as though the victims had somehow brought the murders on themselves.

Peter insisted that this was true and that there was a common link of some kind between the murderers and their victims. This, too, was later verified in the Bugliosi book, although the details Peter related to me were far more explicit.

Of more concern here, however, are the other things he "saw" while working on the case.

Peter had just finished working on the Michigan coed murders, and walked into his house in Studio City on Monday morning (August 11), to be greeted by the ringing of the telephone. It had been ringing all weekend, in fact. Peter Knecht was anxious to get Hurkos on the case.

We met briefly with Knecht the next day (Tuesday) and Peter explained that he would need the co-operation of the police and the principals involved, especially Polanski. He would need permission to visit the murder scene.

On Wednesday night, August 13—a memorable day because of the nation's celebration honoring the moon astronauts—Peter hosted a dinner for a few friends at his favorite Dutch-Indonesian restaurant, Sudi Mampir in Santa Monica. Among his guests were the Jack Albertsons. Jack had won an Academy Award for his role in *The Subject Was Roses*, with Patricia Neal. After dinner we watched the arrival of the astronauts in Los Angeles on a TV set in the restaurant bar. Peter's eighty-five-year-old father from Holland was with us, and Peter was busy translating everything for him in Dutch and explaining how proud he was that America had landed astronauts on the moon.

It was only later that night, on the way home in the Albertsons' station wagon, that the conversation turned to the gruesome murders that all Hollywood was talking about. I was sitting in the front seat between Peter and Jack Albertson, who was driving.

When the Tate murders were mentioned, the first thing Peter said was, "I see there will be a lot of big, very important people in the movies and television and show business mixed up in this case."

The next afternoon (Thursday, August 14) we met again with Peter Knecht in his office. Knecht had invited members of the press. He told them, "Frankly, as far as I'm concerned it's a personal vendetta. I am interested in this case because I was a friend of Jay Sebring's as well as his attorney, and I feel that Peter Hurkos can get a lot more accomplished toward solving this case than the police have done so far."

Soon after the press left, we had two visitors in the office, John and Michelle Phillips, who had been sent as Polanski's emissaries to negotiate with Peter about working on the case, especially regarding admission to the Tate-Polanski murder house.

When Knecht started to introduce them to Peter, John Phillips said, "Mr. Hurkos doesn't need an introduction. I feel it is an honor to be in his presence."

But Peter bristled when John Phillips told him, with some embarrassment, that Polanski had asked him to bring back some proof of Peter's psychic gift before he would give permission for him to visit the murder house in Benedict Canyon.

"I do not have to prove anything," Peter said stubbornly.

Stephy, who had been unusually quiet, suddenly popped to her feet and said, "Peter doesn't have to prove anything to these people. Who are they anyway?"

Peter Knecht, embarrassed, explained, "This is John and Michelle Phillips. I thought you knew them. They were with the Mamas and Papas singing group."

STEPHY: "Who are they?"

KNECHT: "Very big in the record field."

STEPHY: "In that case, if they're so big and if this is such an important case, then I think Peter should be paid for it. After all, he's risking his life and he could be shot and this guy Polanski, whoever he is, wants Peter to prove himself first!"

PETER: "Sit down, Stephy. Be quiet. I don't care what you say, I want to do the case. But I do not have to prove myself here. To nobody!"

Peter Knecht diplomatically suggested that the three of them step into a small inner office for a brief consultation. When they returned, the ruffled feathers had been calmed.

For the record, in spite of Stephy's protests, Peter received not one penny of pay on the Sharon Tate case.

After the brief interruption, Peter looked at John Phillips and said, "It is not only one person, I see at least three or four, maybe six, involved in this murder, and the police are going to find some of them in Canada and the Bahamas."

John Phillips looked frightened. "The Bahamas!" he said. "Yes, I know. And Roman is leaving for the Bahamas on Sunday. I've begged him not to go."

As I listened I thought Peter was probably picking countries out of nowhere. Why did he pick Canada and the Bahamas? But three days later, police questioned, and then released, four suspects in the case, two in Canada and two in the Bahamas. This also was later verified in the Bugliosi book (CHAPTER TITLE: "August 12–15, 1969," page 47), although Bugliosi changed the names for legal reasons. One of them was the Billy whom Peter picked up on so strongly, even to his last name, which a few days later came out in the newspapers as a suspect. He was a former boy friend of Mama Cass Elliot's, was a frequent guest at parties in the Tate residence, once had threatened to strangle a friend of Polanski's, and Polanski had kicked him out. As Bugliosi wrote, "Enraged, Pic* swore, 'I'll kill them all and Voytek will be the first.' "

---

* Pic was the pseudonym that Bugliosi gave to the man Peter called Billy.

Polanski himself would confirm the incident to Peter on tape. On our initial meeting with John and Michelle Phillips in Peter Knecht's office, Peter Hurkos had no way of knowing anything about the suspects in the case except through his psychic impressions. For that matter, he didn't even know who John and Michelle Phillips were until he was told.

Peter was sitting on the other side of the room from Michelle Phillips. He had never set eyes on her before. Suddenly he said, "You have trouble here, left side, in the tubes. I see an operation, but is going to be all right. . . ." He demonstrated by grasping his lower left side. Michelle rose from her chair, open-mouthed and clearly in a state of shock. She staggered over to him, clutching her left side. He began whispering in her ear, and she listened in disbelief as the words tumbled out of his mouth, describing in anatomical detail the reasons for a serious operation he "saw" and its results. I tried to signal him to stop, thinking he was upsetting her too much. But John Phillips turned to me and said, "No, let him go on. She can take it. She's strong."

When Peter finished, Michelle went back to her chair and sat down again, visibly shaken. After she regained her composure, I asked her whether she would mind telling me if what Peter had seen and told her were true.

"It's all true, absolutely true." She paused, then shook her head, still in a daze, and asked, "But how could he possibly know? I only got home from the hospital on Saturday morning—the day this happened."

We met the next day (Friday, August 15) with Roman Polanski at the Phillipses' Bel-Air mansion, which once was the home of singing star Jeanette MacDonald. It is an English Tudor-style mansion decorated with an oriental motif. There were peacocks strutting about the grounds, and an armed security guard at the gate.

Michelle greeted us at the gate, wielding a pearl-handled Belgian pistol for protection. "I even take it into the shower with me. I'm not taking any chances," she said.

Polanski arrived with his entourage, including a private detective assigned to him by Paramount studios as his bodyguard. He seemed to be still doped on tranquilizers and somewhat vague in his reactions. He also was clearly skeptical about Peter's psychic powers, and asked how he came by them. Peter naïvely explained about his fall from the ladder. Polanski cryptically remarked, "Maybe I should fall off a ladder." But he finally consented to allow Peter to go up to the death house the following day.

As we left the Phillipses' house, Polanski walked out to the driveway with us. In a gesture of compassion, Peter put his big hand on Polanski's shoulder, saying, "I know that you are emotionally upset now, but don't worry. When the case is over you will breathe all right again." Then he shook hands with Polanski. I saw him tighten his grip, and then drop it. He blurted out, "Where is the ring?"

"Ring? What ring?"

"The ring that is missing, stolen. The blue ring that you gave your wife," Peter said.

"There was no ring stolen," said Polanski, in his high-pitched whiner's voice. He seemed annoyed.

"There is a ring missing from your wife's finger," Peter insisted. "It is a round ring with bluish lights in an antique setting, and with small stones around it. Here, give me a piece of paper, I draw it for you."

He drew a picture of the ring on the back of an envelope.

Polanski looked at it and then said slowly, as though only now remembering, "Yeah, that's it. Now I remember. I bought it for her in Beverly Hills. It was an opal, surrounded by rubies." He turned away weeping.

I didn't know then but a friend later told me that an opal is a bad-luck sign in witchcraft circles unless it is the person's birthstone. Sharon Tate's birth date was January 24. Her birthstone was a garnet.

Strangely, Sharon's career had been launched with a movie called *13*—a bad-luck number—and ended with one called *13 Chairs* (later changed to *12 Plus 1*. . . . And ironically, one of

Polanski's most successful movies in Europe was one called *Cul de Sac*—about some murders in a big mansion at the end of a cul de sac. The Tate-Polanski house on Cielo Drive in Benedict Canyon was in a wooded, secluded cul de sac, a perfect spot for murder.

And, again ironically, it was only about a mile away from one of Hollywood's most famous "haunted" houses, a house that Sharon and Jay Sebring had shared in their courtship days. It still is known as the Jean Harlow house, and is where Paul Bern committed suicide soon after he married Jean Harlow in 1932. There were stories floating around Hollywood that Sharon Tate had seen Jean Harlow's ghost while occupying the house with Jay Sebring.

Also eerie was the fact that Sharon Tate and Roman Polanski had met during filming of a horror movie called *The Fearless Vampire Killers*.

If Polanski had picked the Benedict Canyon cul de sac as a movie location for one of his typically macabre movies, he could not have chosen a more perfect spot. Nor is it likely that even Polanski, known as movie master of the macabre, could have dreamed up a more bizarre script or cast of characters than those in real life, including himself.

As Peter stepped through that doorway of death, he gasped. He knew instinctively that there was evil here, although as he admitted later, "It didn't need a psychic to know that."

He went from room to room, fingering clothing, bloodstains, furniture. He psychometrized Sharon's rose-colored knit bikini, top and bottom, a dirty girdle, and a shoe. He sat on the bloodstained sofa and began concentrating deeply, sometimes shuddering at what he saw. He was breathing deeply and perspiring heavily.

In Sharon's bedroom he sat on one side of the bed and said, "Someone was sitting here with her when they came in." (COR-RECT: Jay Sebring.)

In the living room again, looking at the beams from which

Sebring's body had hung suspended, he said, "Whips . . . whippings . . ." (CORRECT: one of Sebring's sexual eccentricities.)

Polanski had followed him around, quietly weeping. Peter didn't tell him all he saw, but he did say, "The killers have been at this house before. They were not strangers here." (CORRECT: read Bugliosi.)

Then Peter asked, "Do you know this Billy—Billy———." He gave him the last name.

Polanski replied in a strange tone, "Yes, yes, I know him. He crashed a party at my house about four months ago. He came here with Mama Cass. He was bothering people and I threw him out. Oh yes, he's been here."

Peter asked, "Who is Charlie?" He didn't know. (He had not been there when Sharon saw him.) "Who is David?" He didn't know.

Then Peter, looking up at the loft, suddenly asked a question that was to lead us into a risky net of intrigue.

"Who was the man you invited into this house who is an artist, a painter?"

"A painter? I don't know any painter. Oh, I suppose there was a man in this house painting the walls or the loft, I don't know," Polanski said vaguely.

"No, no, no. I do not mean a house painter. I mean an artist, not a portrait painter. He paints abstracts, all kinds of different designs, lines, stripes, sharp colors," Peter explained.

No, Polanski said, he didn't know any abstract painter.

Did he know someone by the name of Kabaleski, or Kaveleski, or Kobolefski, asked Peter, trying several pronunciations of a name that was coming in strong to him. No, he did not, Polanski replied. Peter then asked to go up into the loft.

As they climbed the ladder to the loft, Peter asked, "Who is Vito, Vito? Is he a painter?" Polanski nodded his head, no. He seemed very tired, and so was Peter by now.

They came back down the ladder, and Polanski wandered off into Sharon's bedroom again. Presently he came out with something clutched in his hand.

Peter's mind was still on the artist.

"I want to see this man tomorrow," he said. "I mean the artist who was here. It is very important."

Polanski surprised us by saying with a resigned sigh, and in a tone suggesting that he was tired of the subject, "You can meet him today if you want."

It is still all there on our tapes.

Why had Polanski denied knowing the painter in the loft?

Peter said he was too tired to work any more today and would prefer to see the painter next day when he could start fresh. As he started toward the door, Polanski came over to him and opened his hand. In his palm was an antique ring—an opal surrounded by rubies. It was the same ring Peter had described to him when he told Polanski that it was missing from his wife's finger.

But why had Sharon not been wearing the ring the night she was killed? . . . Had she taken it off before the ritual, following the ancient black magic custom of removing jewelry? Or had someone familiar with black magic and witchcraft told Sharon that an opal is bad luck unless it is your own birthstone?

Peter was mumbling those strange names again to Polanski. Vito, Vito, Vito. Kavaleski, Kabaleski, Kobolefski. "I have to see this man, this artist. He knows something important about the murders," Peter said.

Finally, Polanski, muttering that he didn't know what was going on in his house while he was away, picked up the telephone and dialed a number in Malibu. He carried on a conversation in Polish. Then he turned to Peter and said, "The artist's gallery is on Wilshire Boulevard in Beverly Hills. We can go there tomorrow."

When Peter came out of the house on Cielo Drive in Benedict Canyon he told us again, "Three people that did it. . . . Charlie, with beard, lives in mountain area, little guy and big skinny guy . . . hippie types . . . freaky . . . in dope . . . all these people, lots of people involved. . . ."

At that exact moment, Charlie with beard (Manson) and family were grubbing it out at the now well-known Spahn Ranch in Topanga Canyon, practically right under the LAPD's nose.

On Monday, August 18, Peter and Stephany and I met with Peter Knecht at the Beverly Hills Brown Derby for lunch, and then proceeded to our two o'clock appointment at 9406 Wilshire Boulevard.

It was the address of a small art gallery, and I had a spine-tingling feeling as we walked in. There was something eerie about it, for it was almost too precisely as Peter had described it, as though he had been there before. And yet I knew he had not. The walls were hung with abstract paintings—and only abstracts. No others.

I noticed the signature on the paintings: Witold K. No last name. I'm sure that Peter didn't even notice the signature. Witold K. Probably pronounced like Vito, with a soft V.

It wasn't until weeks later that I learned his real name, which he had left behind him in Poland. It was Wintact Kazerowski. Bugliosi says it was Witold Kaczanowski. Whichever, it obviously was the name that Peter had been groping for—and he wasn't too far off.

Witold, we were to learn later, was one of the principals in the Tate-Sebring investigation, an informant who had given police valuable information, including names of at least three persons who, he said, were actively involved in the bloodletting at the $1,000-per-month rental home of the Polanskis. He told police that he believed he knew the killer or killers responsible for the massacre, and he was given around-the-clock police guard for protection of his life.

Witold, also a Polish émigré and a friend of Frykowski's, was invited to the fateful party at the Tate-Polanski estate, but he had to work late that night and so escaped the fate of the slain five. He presumably supplied to police the names of several persons who either had a role in the killings or some knowledge of the crime. One person named by him was an aspiring Hollywood actor, known chiefly to industry figures but unfamiliar to the movie-going public. As an informant, Witold's story to the police had followed this line: He was a close friend of Polanski's in Poland, had come to this country two years ago, met Abigail Folger in New York and her Polish lover, Frykowski, and had seen them frequently since they moved to California. Miss Folger, he said, had supplied Frykowski with funds for his drug habit (in an attempt to hold him when he became interested in another woman), and cocaine deliveries were made to the Tate-Polanski residence while the Polanskis were in Europe, he said.

We had none of this information when we went to visit Witold in his studio. It was all to be reported later in the newspapers, but all Peter had to go on was what he had seen and felt at the death house.

Roman Polanski was there waiting for us in the art gallery, with his usual entourage. The place seemed to be swarming with policemen, both inside and out. Witold was a tall, slender young man with curly brown hair and a terribly frightened look on his finely chiseled face. He barely spoke English, and in the confusion of all the introductions, I had the distinct impression that Polanski and Witold were certainly not strangers, although for some reason they wished us to think they were.

The interview was held in a tiny cubicle off the front gallery, and it was between Peter, Polanski, and Witold, with Stephany at the tape recorder. When Peter Knecht and I started to move in closer where we could listen, Polanski curtly ordered us back. So we stayed in the gallery, and my knowledge of what transpired comes from a couple of Polish translators whom I hired to help us with the tape transcriptions. Polanski acted as translator between Peter and Witold.

Peter did not ask many questions. First, "Were you ever in his house?" meaning Polanski's.

Polanski translated: "Were you in my house while I was away?"

There was a mumbling exchange of words that was indistinguishable.

"You know Billy. What do you think of Billy?"

Silence. Then quietly seething: "Completely paranoiac. He is a man capable of killing in his paranoiac state." (He's the one who tried to kill Witold at a Polanski party.)

Then a curious thing happened on our tape recorder as our Polish translators were translating. It was obvious that there was a little repartee going on between Polanski and Witold, which Peter was not supposed to understand. Our translators asked for another playback of that portion of the tape, and then another, and another. They wanted to be very sure.

What they heard was Witold, in a low, seething voice, saying under his breath to Polanski, "You can talk me into anything."

What did it mean?

Peter's next question to Witold: "When was the last time you saw his wife?" (Meaning Sharon)

Polanski spoke to Witold in Polish, and then replied to Peter in English, "He never saw her. He spoke to her on the phone only. He never saw her in his life. My wife? He never saw my wife. . . ."

"But he was in the house," Peter said.

"Yeah, but that was when my wife was in Europe." He asked Witold, "Did you stay over in the house when I was gone?" And then he answered his own question, "Yeah, he was many times in the house. He was sleeping there even. . . ."

Again there was the mumbling between them.

"Was he painting in the house?" Peter asked.

"Yeah, he did paint there many times. . . . But so what?" Polanski said.

Peter asked about Billy again. "Did you ever have any trouble with Billy?" More Polish translation. Then, "Yeah, he had trouble—the usual thing. Of course he had trouble. Billy was shouting and screaming at him, 'I'm going to kill you.' Many times. But he didn't pay any notice. . . ."

Our Polish translators were convinced that Polanski and Witold were not strangers, that they were friends who had known one another for some time. They used the familiar Polish term *ty* for you, instead of the more formal term *pan*, meaning "sir" in

Polish. Their speech was very informal, indicating that they were definitely not strangers. . . . As it turned out, Polanski's first wife, a Polish actress, at one time was Witold's girl friend. . . . And the night of the Tate murders Witold had gone to John Phillips' house after work—instead of to the Tate-Polanski house where he had been invited.

Why did Polanski at first deny to Peter that he knew an abstract painter named Vito—or Witold? This would come under the category of post-mortem speculation on a case that has now been solved.

More significant is Peter's degree of accuracy in so many details —people, places, and circumstances that he could know nothing about except through psychic insight: the fact that he knew there was an artist in the loft when Polanski was denying it, that he knew (almost) his name, that he knew certain suspects (one of whom he named specifically) would be picked up in the Bahamas and Canada, that he knew the murderers had been to the Polanski-Tate house before, and that he knew the murders were masterminded by a little guy named Charlie who lived just over the hill in Topanga Canyon.

On the last page of one of my notebooks is the notation (from Peter Knecht) "Chief of police was very impressed. Following up Peter's leads. Issuing all points for Charlie and Bill and David."

Then Peter was dropped from the case and warned: Hands off! It was an about-switch from the co-operation he at first had with the LAPD—and possibly the highest tribute that could be paid to his powers as a psychic.